Whimsical One-Step Appliqué and Quilting

Tonee White

That Patchwork Place®

Dedication

To my husband, Bob, for giving me "my turn."

Acknowledgments

Thanks go to:

Deborah Goldman, my first quilting teacher, for introducing me to the "quilt world;"

all my students for their support and encouragement to believe in myself;

Kerry Hoffman and Barbara Weiland for their infectious enthusiasm for my work.

Credits

Editor-in-Chief . . . . Barbara Weiland
Technical Editor . . . . Kerry I. Hoffman
Managing Editor . . . . Greg Sharp
Copy Editor . . . . Liz McGehee
Proofreader . . . . .Tina Cook
Text and Cover Design . . . . Kay Green
Typesetting . . . . Julianna Reynolds
Photography . . . . .Brent Kane
Illustration and Graphics . . . . Laurel Strand
Stephanie Benson
Barb Tourtillotte

Appliquilt!™ Whimsical One-Step Appliqué and Quilting©
© 1994 by Tonee White

That Patchwork Place, Inc.,
PO Box 118,
Bothell, WA 98041-0118
USA

The information in this book is presented in good faith, but no warranty is given nor results guaranteed. Since That Patchwork Place, Inc., has no control over choice of materials or procedures, the company assumes no responsibility for the use of this information.

Printed in the United States of America
99 98 97 96 95   6 5 4

White, Tonee,
    Appliquilt! : one-step appliqué and quilting / Tonee White.
       p.   cm.
    ISBN 1-56477-052-4 :
       1. Appliqué—Patterns. 2. Quilting—Patterns. I. Title.
TT779.W55 1994
746.9'7—dc20   93-38573
                                                    CIP

Contents

Meet the Author

Tonee White's first quilting class four years ago hooked her on quilting. Unable to buy as many quilts as she wanted or find the designs and colors of her choice, Tonee decided to make her own.

Tonee is not new to handwork, having done needlepoint for twenty years and cross-stitch for five. But she says, "I have never found a creative outlet like quilting!"

Her original designs, ranging from whimsical to primitive, are quick and easy to make. Her method of combining appliqué and quilting all in one step is a real time-saver. She now teaches classes and encourages others to use their creativity when making their own quilts.

Tonee spends the other part of her life as a registered nurse, working in the delivery room. Living in Irvine, California, she is happily married and has seven children and one grandchild. Her family enthusiastically supports her newfound quilting interest.

Introduction

Originally, quilts were made primarily for warmth, using feed sacks and scraps of fabric from worn-out clothing. While making these utility quilts, pioneer women practiced the ultimate in recycling.

Today, quilting can be anything from a hobby or recreation to a sophisticated art form. Displays of impressive quilts can now be found in the most notable art galleries and museums.

While taking quilting classes and then while teaching, I observed a distressing phenomenon. Students spent a great deal of time, effort, and money to engage in this craft and were nervous about making every seam exact and following a pattern precisely. They were not enjoying themselves. As a result, I urge my students to relax and not feel pressured to make every seam exact or each piece meet its neighbor at the precise point called for in the pattern. Self-expression and experimentation are encouraged. Students are also encouraged to understand that a mistake can sometimes bring out a great new idea.

Appliqué, in particular, can bring on sweaty palms and choruses of "I can't do that" or "I don't like the 'A' word." That's why I came up with a one-step method of appliquéing and quilting pattern shapes to a quilt top that is already "sandwiched" with the batting and backing. What makes this even better is that pinking shears are used to cut out the pattern shapes and you do not turn under the edges of the pattern pieces as you stitch! Appliqué and quilting are completed in one step, hence the term appliquilt!

Developing designs for this method was and continues to be a delight. My taste runs from the primitive and whimsical to more traditional patterns. A Baltimore Album quilt may not seem to be an appropriate design for this method, but I'm working on it.

I hope the designs in this book inspire you to use the creativity I feel certain all of you have. Most of all, I hope you toss aside some of the notions of "how it should be done" and just have fun making these quilts and all of the quilts that you design.

There are enough rules in our lives that we must follow. Use quilting as your vehicle to express yourself in a happy and enjoyable way. Trust your instincts. If you like the colors you've chosen, then use them! You're the one who will live with your creations, so you have to please yourself.

Materials & Tools

Fabrics

While selecting fabrics for your stress-free appliquilt projects, keep in mind that you will be sewing through at least four layers: the pattern shape, quilt top, batting, and backing. For this reason, the easier the fabric is to "needle," the easier your sewing will be.

Soft cottons, muslin, and many wonderful woven fabrics that are so popular now needle like butter. Stiffer fabrics like chintzes and batiks are more difficult to needle and therefore take longer to stitch. By all means, use any fabric that will make your quilt as wonderful as it can be. Anything you can put a needle through will work, but remember that some fabrics are easier to needle than others.

I used tea-dyed fabrics for many of the quilts in this book for a primitive or aged appearance. Try the following recipe if you would like to do the same.

Recipe for Tea Dyeing

1 quart hot tap water
3 tablespoons instant coffee
8 tea bags

Stir instant coffee into water. Let the tea bags steep in the mixture for a few minutes; remove tea bags and soak prewashed fabric in the tea dye for 20 minutes. Soak longer or even overnight to get darker results. To get a blotchy effect, leave the tea bags in the water with the fabric. The more you experiment with tea-dyeing your fabrics, the more you will be able to predict the results.

Supplies

Embellishments

The buttons, trinkets, bits of lace, ribbons, and other decorations used on these quilts add greatly to their charm. I collect all kinds of these items. I don't always know how I will use them when I buy them, but I know they will eventually find their way onto one of my creations.

Local craft, quilt, fabric, and antique shops may be good sources for embellishments. If you have difficulty finding the embellishment gems that I have used, refer to the "Resource List" on page 16.

Batting

I use Pellon™ fleece almost exclusively in my appliquilts, and occasionally, I use one or two layers of cotton flannel, although flannel is harder to needle. A thin batting works well for these quilts because they are used primarily as wall hangings or table toppers.

Thread

Almost any kind of thread or stitching medium will do as long as it is strong enough to hold the layers together. Experiment with different threads to find the ones that are easiest to use and that achieve the look you want.

I use #8 perle cotton for almost everything. Its strands are twisted together so that the threads don't separate, and it pulls through the "sandwich" very easily. It is also available in many colors and shades. For some projects, a heavier-weight (#3) perle cotton is used to attach embellishments.

You may use three to six strands of embroidery floss, but the strands may separate or knot a little, giving an uneven look. Heavy-duty quilting thread does not show as well as the floss or perle cotton.

For most of the projects in this book, I stitched with perle cotton or floss in a contrasting color. This adds to the homespun look, creates visual interest, and helps define shapes. This is especially true if there is little contrast between the designs and the background fabric. For a more refined look, try a quilting thread in the same color as the pattern piece.

For machine quilting, I use invisible nylon thread in my needle, and cotton thread to match the backing fabric in my bobbin. This eliminates the need to make a decision about thread color because the thread really cannot be seen.

Scissors

I cut out the pattern shapes for all the quilts in this book with scalloping shears. The traditional sawtooth pinking shears work well, also.

Keep in mind that the sawtooth and scalloping shears take a wider swipe than regular scissors. Cutting out a small piece, such as a hand or foot, the exact same size as the template pattern might be a little difficult. Don't worry about it. If it's stitched to the end of an arm or a leg, it's going to look like a hand or a foot.

To keep your fabric scissors sharp, do not use them to cut out paper templates. Use a separate pair for cutting paper and template plastic.

Needles

Number 5 embroidery needles work best for me. They are thin, yet the eye is large enough to accommodate the perle cotton or floss.

Small chenille needles will work but are larger and therefore create more "drag" when going through the layers of the quilt.

Experiment with the needles you have. The two things to consider are "Is the eye large enough?" and "Is the needle sharp enough?"

Making the Quilt Sandwich Foundation

Quilting and appliqué in one step requires that you make the "quilt sandwich" or foundation first. To do this, the three layers of the quilt—top, batting, and backing—must be prepared and pinned or hand basted together. The quilt is then ready for appliquilting or for some preliminary quilting.

Cut the backing 1"–2" larger than the top on all sides. With the wrong side of the backing face up, tape it to a hard, flat surface, such as a table or floor. Secure the fabric so that it is smooth and fairly taut, but do not stretch it out of shape. Cut the batting to the same size as your backing. Lay the batting on top of the backing and smooth it out, working from the center out to the edges.

Next, add the background fabric or pieced top, smoothing it from the center outward. Pin-baste your quilt. (I prefer medium-sized safety pins.) Or, baste with needle and thread, pinning or stitching every 4"–6". Start from the center and work out to the edges of the quilt.

Always smooth each time you pin or take a stitch. Do not close the pins until all are in place. This helps keep your sandwich flat. If you close each pin as you go, it may shift the backing slightly, and by the time you have pinned your last pin, the backing has shifted quite a bit.

Some of the quilts in this book require hand or machine quilting "in-the-ditch" to help keep the sandwich from shifting while you appliquilt. If you choose to quilt by hand, use either quilting thread or perle cotton and use a running stitch. I machine quilt in-the-ditch with invisible nylon thread in my needle and cotton thread in my bobbin.

You are now ready to appliqué the shapes to the top and quilt in one easy step—let the appliquilting begin!

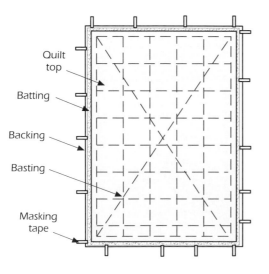

Quilt top
Batting
Backing
Basting
Masking tape

Cutting Out the Pattern Pieces

For the quilts in this book, you must make cutting templates and, in some cases, tracing templates. Tracing is easier and ensures an accurate pattern when you make templates from template plastic. The stiffness allows you to trace much more accurately than is possible with a paper template.

Trace all pattern pieces onto the template plastic with a sharp pencil or fine-tip permanent marking pen. It's a good idea to mark the right side of the template with the name of the piece. Cut the templates out, using your paper scissors instead of your fabric scissors.

To make the design exactly as it is pictured on the page, place the templates face down on the wrong side of the fabric. To make a reverse image of the design figure, place the templates right side up on the wrong side of the fabric. Cut out the pattern shapes from the fabric on the traced line. Do **not** add seam allowances to the pieces; the templates are actual size.

If you use a marking pen with disappearing ink and you feel confident the ink will disappear, trace on the right side of your fabric. If you use this method, you do not need to reverse the template.

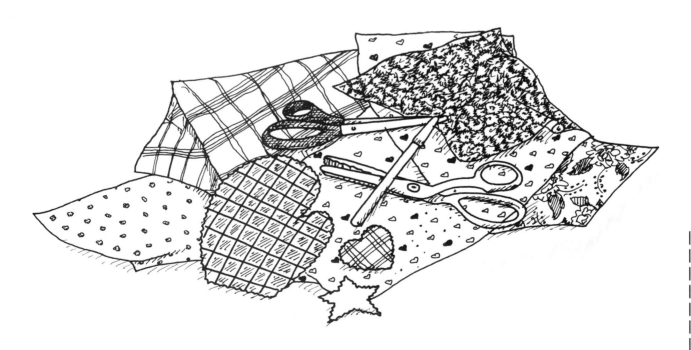

Appliquilting—
Appliqué & Quilting in One Step

After pinning the pattern shapes to your quilt sandwich, you are ready to stitch. By stitching the shapes to the quilt through all of the layers, your quilt is appliquéd and quilted at the same time!

The other aspect that makes these quilts so inviting and stress-free is that you use a running stitch to appliqué and quilt.

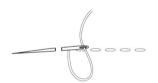

Running Stitch

You can make the stitches as long or short as you wish. You don't even have to draw a stitching line. I usually follow the inside edge of the pattern shapes and start my stitching on the top side of the quilt, leaving the knot on top. When I finish my stitching or come to the end of the thread, I end on the top side and tie one or two knots.

Sometimes I use a square knot, too. Leaving the knots on top adds to the charm of the quilts and makes them look more rustic.

Another method that I like is to begin and end the stitching at the same place, tying both thread ends together in one knot. Working from the top of the quilt, start stitching through all the layers, leaving a 4"- to 6"-long tail as shown. Continue stitching, working your way back to where you started. End your stitching on the top and tie the two ends together in a square knot (right over left and under, then left over right and under). Clip the ends, leaving a ¼"-long tail.

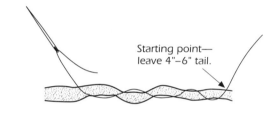

Starting point—
leave 4"–6" tail.

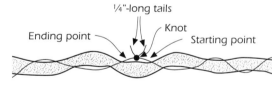

¼"-long tails

Ending point   Knot   Starting point

Knot and trim to ¼"-long tails.

Some of the quilts call for machine quilting on the seam lines or in-the-ditch through all the layers to keep the quilt sandwich from shifting. A walking foot or even-feed foot helps all the layers of the quilt sandwich move pucker-free through the machine. You may also quilt in-the-ditch by hand with perle cotton, using a running stitch.

Binding

Cut 1¼"- to 1½"-wide binding strips with pinking shears. Fold the strips in half lengthwise and, with wrong sides together, press. After you have trimmed the batting and backing to match the quilt top, wrap the binding strip around the edge of the quilt.

Using perle cotton, stitch through all the layers, ¼" from the inside edge of the binding. Use the same running stitch you used for the appliquilting. Miter the corners as you come to them by folding and pinning.

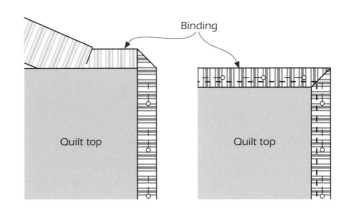

Some of the quilt projects were bound before being appliquilted, and others were bound in the final step. You can develop your own method and style. On larger quilts, you may use a more traditional binding method, but this simple binding works well for any wall hanging, regardless of size.

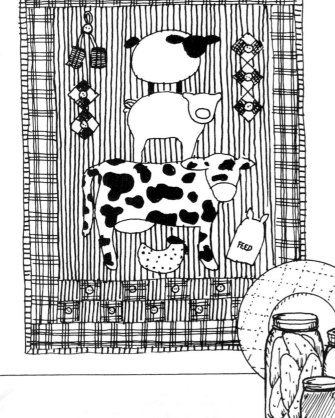

Adding Embellishments

When sewing buttons onto my quilts, I use perle cotton or embroidery floss and start from the top side of the quilt, leaving a 4"- to 6"-long tail. Stitch through the holes in the buttons twice and tie a double knot to secure. Clip the tails to the desired length. I use the same method for applying beads, charms, lace, and most other embellishments.

When attaching something that does not have holes, cut a 12" length of perle cotton and glue the midpoint of the perle cotton to the back of the object. With a needle, pull both ends of the perle cotton through the top of the quilt to the back and tie the ends together.

Another option is to add a ribbon bow with buttons sewn to the end of the ribbon. This adds color, dimension, and texture. Experiment with silk flowers, leaves, or anything else you have. Have fun with this!

Embroidery stitches add another interesting textural touch to your quilts. I have used French knots, crow footing, and the stem stitch.

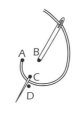

Go through all layers.

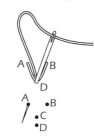

Travel through top layer only.

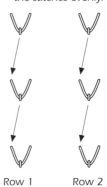

Work in rows, spacing the stitches evenly.

Row 1   Row 2

Crow Footing

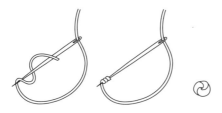

French Knot

Stem Stitch

Adapting Traditional Patterns

Use this easy, stress-free method of appliqué and quilting in one step for almost any appliqué project. Simply cut out the pattern shapes with pinking shears and eliminate the seam allowance. The look of your finished quilt will be unique and whimsical.

Try some of the more traditional pieced blocks. Take a look at the quilts in the photographs, beginning on page 17. Have you always been afraid to make Grandmother's Flower Garden, thinking that it was too difficult? It is really very easy!

Cut out all the hexagons in the size that you want with pinking shears. Pin them on a sandwiched foundation, then stitch through all the layers, using a running stitch and perle cotton. Overlap the edges slightly if you do not want the background to show. There are no corners to match other than to lay them together properly before they are sewn. It's fast and easy. I can't think of a traditional pieced block that cannot be made using this method.

Rubber Stamping Quilt Blocks

Creative rubber stamping is enjoying a popular resurgence. Many stores are specializing in these little rubber gems. I am drawn to stamps for the design possibilities and because they are cute. I can't put much effort into creating, stamping, embossing, and coloring a project for a greeting card, wrapping paper, or mailer. These items, although appreciated by the receiver, usually end up in the receiver's drawer or even their wastebasket. I like creating more lasting items and, being a quilter, the idea for these small wall hangings was born. Photographs of rubber-stamp quilts begin on page 26.

I realized that I had potential themes for my little quilts when I was categorizing my stamps for storage. Coordinated embellishments and old buttons soon found their way onto these wall hangings, too.

Selecting Fabrics for Stamping

When choosing fabrics on which to stamp, pay attention to thread count. The tighter the weave or higher the thread count, the less likely your ink or paint will bleed. I use good-quality muslin for the projects that call for it.

Solid-colored fabrics work well, but the color of the fabric may dictate the ink and paint colors that you apply. Try your pens or paints on a scrap first to see how the colors look together.

If you use a looser-weave fabric, stamp it with less ink from the pad, use a pen that has dried out a bit, or use less paint on your brush. Pencils do not pose bleeding problems but may stretch the fabric if too much pressure is applied.

Choosing Your Stamps

Stamped imprints are not as sharp on fabric as they are on paper, and some rubber stamps work better than others. Ink adheres best to stamps that have deep cuts and sharp ridges of rubber. Images that are mostly outlined and that have few or very small, flat areas also work well. Large areas of flat or smooth surfaces are less desirable since they tend to smudge on your fabric.

Most shops are happy to provide a demonstration. Take along a piece of fabric and ask the clerk to try your choices. This helps you to see how each stamp looks on fabric.

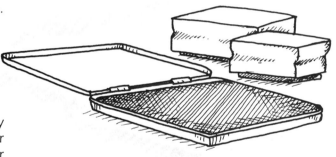

Testing Inks and Ink Pads

Some ink pads on the market are advertised as "permanent." Buyers beware! I have found that some of these inks bleed when wet. I've discovered that non-permanent inks, when heat-set, hold up beautifully to dampness or even total immersion in water. Test your stamp-pad inks by stamping an impression on fabric. Heat set with an iron on the cotton/linen setting for ten seconds. Use a press cloth to protect the bottom of the iron. Immerse the piece of fabric in water. If the color does not run, the ink should work well. This may not mean, however, that different colors of the same brand will react the same way. Test each color ink that you plan to use.

Adding Color to Stamped Designs

I enjoy coloring my stamped designs. Not only does color add definition to the design, but it can complement the colors of the background fabric. You can add color with pens, pencils, and paints.

The fabric pens now available work well for me. They have two different tips—a brush type that I like to use for coloring larger areas and a pointed tip that is great for small areas or for outlining. When heat-set as described above, the color holds well. Again, it is always wise to test each pen for color-fastness.

Some pens are "wetter" than others. If the pen delivers too much ink, the ink may travel along the fabric fibers and bleed. If this occurs, leave the cap off the pen for an hour (or overnight if necessary) and test it again.

For a nice soft look, try colored pencils. Because the color is not absorbed into the fabric as it is with pens, a pastel look results. Use a light touch when coloring with a pencil, to avoid stretching the fabric.

Fabric paint is also a good medium to use. It takes longer to dry; therefore, it will take you longer to complete the project. When coloring with pens or painting adjacent areas with different colors, allow one area to dry before coloring in the other, or the paint may bleed.

Because I have not found a satisfactory white pen, I use white paint on the areas I want to be white. When stamping on white fabric or muslin, many areas that I want to be white are left uncolored. But on snowmen or ghosts, for example, I use a small brush to apply white paint inside the design lines.

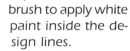

Planning Your Stamped Project

As I mentioned before, design themes or subjects develop from the stamps you have on hand. You can use a favorite stamp and build from it. For example, if you have a stamp that features an apple with stars, you could follow a patriotic theme and include stamps with flags, Uncle Sam, and a map of the United States. Or, you could go off in another direction and include other apple stamps. Yet another theme might include other fruits or a combination of fruits and vegetables. The design possibilities are endless, and the creativity they stir up is wonderful.

While designing your quilt, consider using multiples of the same stamp in a row or some other formation. A row or column of the same stamped design adds interest. Stamp your selected designs on fabric pieces that have been cut with pinking shears or torn.

The size of your quilt depends on your overall design and the number of stamps and embellishments that you use. You may want to make your first stress-free quilt a fat-quarter size (18" x 22").

Arrange your stamped pieces on the background fabric. Pin in place. Be sure to leave spaces for embellishments, such as charms, bits of lace or fabrics, buttons, trinkets, beads, or ribbon. Ideas for embellishments are on page 6.

Assembling Your Stamped Project

Once you have completed your quilt design, you are ready to assemble it.

Cut the backing and batting 1"–2" larger than the quilt top. Pin the stamped fabric pieces and embellishments to the background piece. Carefully place the background piece on the batting, centering it. Repin your arrangements through all the layers—background, batting, and backing. (See page 8.)

Following the stitching directions that begin on page 10, sew your stamped fabrics and embellishments to the quilt.

Bind the quilt, following directions on page 11.

Laundering Appliquilts

I've been asked if it is safe to launder these little quilts. If your knots have been tied securely, they can be laundered with care. Wash them by hand or in the machine on the gentle cycle and air dry on a flat surface. Do not hang to dry, as they will stretch out of shape. The edges may curl up a bit, but they can be pressed flat. You may find you like the "curly" look. I have left them as is on a few pieces, such as flowers and leaves. It adds dimension to a design.

Resource List

Rubber Stamps

The rubber stamp designs found on the rubber-stamp quilts were created by the following companies:

All Night Media, Inc.
Alias Smith & Rowe
Ann-ticipations
Delafield Stamp Company
Good Stamps - Stamp Goods
Hero Arts Rubber Stamps, Inc.
Imaginations!
Imagine That (Uptown Rubber Stamp, Inc.)
INKADINKADO, Inc.
Mostly Animals Corporation
Museum of Modern Rubber
Posh Impressions®
Printworks Collection
Rubber Stamps of America
Stampa Barbara
Stampendous, Inc.™
Timeless Images
Works of Heart

Embellishments

Some of the items included on my quilts can be purchased from the following suppliers:

A Homespun Heart
2223 F Street
Iowa City, Iowa 52245
(800) 336-3490
Apple-tree button, snowman button

Fibre Craft
Niles, Illinois 60648
Garden tools

The Wonderful, Whimsical Appliquilts

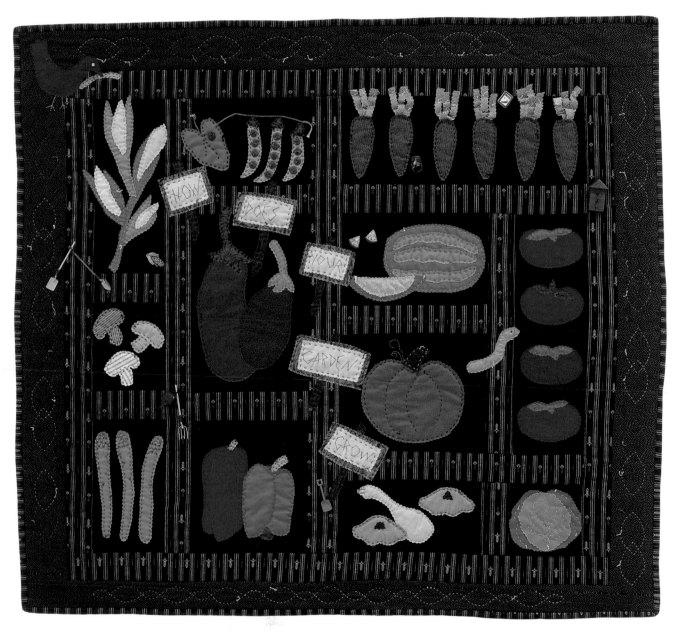

"How Does Your Garden Grow?" by Tonee White, 1993, Irvine, California, 44" x 41". This garden grows very well with large, brightly colored fruits and vegetables, set off by a dark background.

"Bunnies and Carrots" by Tonee White, 1993, Irvine, California, 22" x 22". Bunnies and carrots and even a bunny pull-toy will delight a child at Easter or anytime.

"Hearts 'n' Hands" by Tonee White, 1993, Irvine, California, 28" x 28". Buttons, hearts, and old-fashioned stitching in this little quilt is reminiscent of Victorian times.

"Sunflowers and Crows" by Tonee White, 1993, Irvine, California, 30" x 40". Crows bask in the sun while sunflowers grow in the dark brown soil.

"Animal Stack" by Tonee White, 1993, Irvine, California, 26" x 36". Hay bales, barnyard animals, and Four Patch squares in plaids and checks create a "down-home" look.

"Mittens and Snowmen" by Tonee White, 1992, Irvine, California, 28" x 36". Winter is here in this fun-to-make quilt. The mittens are drying on the line after creating these two wonderful snowmen.

"God Bless America" by Tonee White, 1993, Irvine, California, 28" x 38". A girl and her dog salute Old Glory.
Making this quilt could also be a geography lesson as most state capitals are represented by a small red bead.

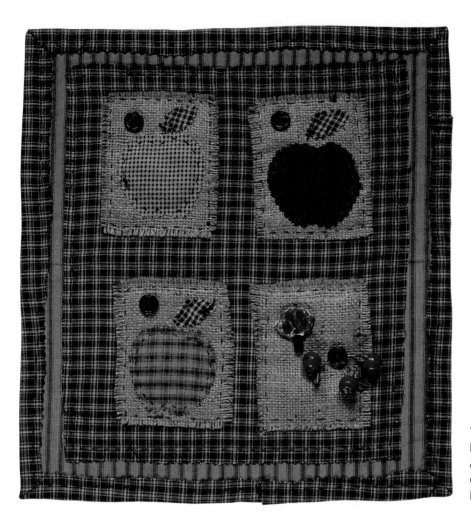

"Apples" by Tonee White, 1993, Irvine, California, 12" x 14". This quick-and-easy little wall hanging can be completed in an afternoon. The embellishments add a special charm.

"My, My, Apple Pie" by Tonee White, 1992, Irvine, California, 12" x 15". Outlined apples highlight the background for this small, portable project. You'll finish it in no time.

Adapting Traditional Patterns

Don't let seemingly intricate traditional quilt-block patterns hold you back—just make them the stress-free appliquilt way!

"Nine Block Sampler" by Tonee White, 1993, Irvine, California, 40" x 40". The author used her stress-free appliquilting method to make all of these traditional, pieced blocks.

"Grandmother's Flower Garden" by Tonee White, 1993, Irvine, California, 17" x 18". This popular pattern is somewhat difficult to execute in the traditional way, but it is easy to appliquilt.

Rubber Stamp Quilts

Rubber Stamp Wall Hangings by Tonee White, 1992–1993, Irvine, California, in sizes ranging from 14" x 14" to 22" x 22". Examples are of rubber-stamp quilts done in different themes. Notice the embellishments and the arrangement of the stamped pieces.

"Sunflowers"

Rubber stamps from Stampendous, Inc.™, All Night Media©, Mostly Animals Corporation©.

"Heart"

Rubber stamps from Imagine That© (Uptown Rubber Stamp, Inc.),Annette Watkins©, Museum of Modern Rubber©, Works of Heart©

"Halloween"

Rubber stamps from Rubber Stamps of America©, Posh Impressions©, Museum of Modern Rubber©, Stampa Barbara©, Delafield Stamp Company.©, Stamp-endous, Inc.™, Timeless Images©, Good Stamps©, and Mostly Animals Corporation©

"Harvest"

Rubber stamps from Timeless Images©, Delafield Stamp Company©, Rubber Stamps of America©, Imaginations!©, Posh Impressions©, Stampendous, Inc.™

"Snowmen"

Rubber stamps from Good Stamps©, Imagine That© (Uptown Rubber Stamp, Inc.) Museum of Modern Rubber©, Stampendous, Inc.™

"Christmas"

Rubber stamps from Museum of Modern Rubber©, Posh Impressions©, Imagine That© (Uptown Rubber Stamp, Inc.), Alias Smith & Rowe©, Mostly Animals©, Stampendous, Inc.™, Hero Arts Rubber Stamps, Inc.©, and INKA-DINKADO©

Apples

This homespun quilt includes crisp apples (even a green one) and would be perfect hanging in a kitchen or breakfast room.

Color Photo: page 24
Size: 12" x 14"
Materials: 44"-wide fabric

¹⁄₃ yd. green ticking for background and backing

¹⁄₃ yd. red plaid for foundation and binding

¹⁄₈ yd. tan burlap for base behind apples

Scraps: red plaid or red-striped fabric for apple
   green for apple and leaves

14" x 16" piece of Pellon or other thin batting

#8 perle cotton in red, green, and other assorted
   colors

Red buttons, apple-tree button, and small red apple
   charms

Making the Foundation

Cutting

From the green ticking, cut:
   2 rectangles, each 12" x 14"

From the red plaid, cut:
   1 rectangle, 9¹⁄₂" x 11¹⁄₂"

Directions

   Layer the batting between the two 12" x 14" green rectangles. One side will be your quilt top and the other will be the backing. Pin-baste the edges. See "Making the Quilt Sandwich Foundation" on page 8.

Appliquilt

Use templates on this page.

1. Center and pin-baste the red 9½" x 11½" rectangle on the quilt-top side. With a contrasting color of perle cotton, stitch it to the foundation by sewing through all of the layers, ¼" inside the outer edge. See Appliquilting directions on page 10.
2. From tan burlap, cut 4 rectangles, each 3½" x 4½".
3. Place the 4 pieces of burlap on the quilt and pin in place. Refer to the Quilt Plan for placement. Stitch with a contrasting color of perle cotton.

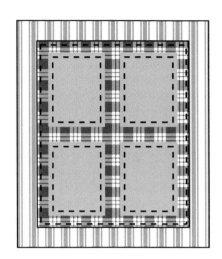

4. Make plastic templates for the apples and leaves, following the directions on page 9.
5. From the red scraps, cut 2 apples and, from the green scraps, cut 1 apple and 3 leaves. Stitch them to the burlap rectangles. Use red perle cotton to stitch the leaves and the green apple, and green perle cotton to stitch the red apples.
6. After the burlap is stitched in place, fray the edges by removing 2 or 3 threads on each side of each rectangle.

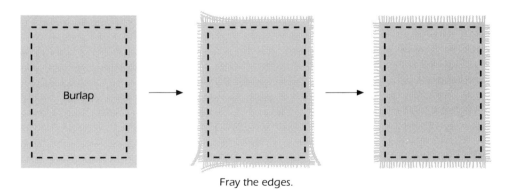

Fray the edges.

Embellishments and Finishing

1. Sew 1 red button in each of the rectangles that have apples. See page 12.
2. Sew the apple charms in the lower right burlap rectangle. Sew a red button to cover the spot where you attached the apple charms. See "Adding Embellishments" on page 12. Sew the apple-tree button to the same block.
3. Cut 1½"-wide binding strips from the red plaid. Bind the edges, following directions on page 11.

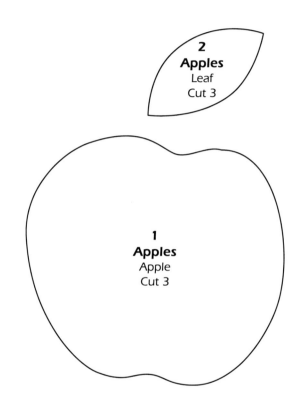

2
Apples
Leaf
Cut 3

1
Apples
Apple
Cut 3

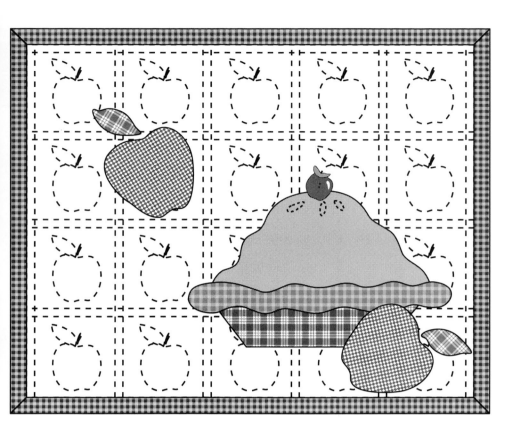

My, My, Apple Pie

Look what you can do with a fat quarter of muslin. This is a great portable project to take along anywhere, and you'll finish it in no time!

Color Photo: page 24
Size: 12" x 14"
Materials: 44"-wide fabric

$^1/_2$ yd. muslin for background and backing

Scraps: red for apples
　　　　green for leaves
　　　　blue for pie dish
　　　　tan checked fabric for pie crust
　　　　tea-dyed muslin for pie top (See the tea-dyeing recipe on page 6.)

$^1/_8$ yd. blue checked fabric or fabric scraps for binding

16" x 18" piece of Pellon fleece or other thin batting

#8 perle cotton in assorted colors, including black, red, and green

Apple button

Making the Foundation

1. From the muslin, cut 2 rectangles, each 12" x 15".
2. On one of the muslin rectangles, draw a grid as shown on the Grid Diagram (page 32) with light pencil lines, using a 15"-long clear plastic ruler. The long sides of the rectangle are the top and bottom. Draw the first vertical line 1$^1/_4$" from the left of the center. Draw the first horizontal line through the center of the quilt. Continue drawing the remaining lines to complete all of the squares. The squares measure 2$^1/_2$" x 2$^1/_2$", and there are two lines between each square, $^1/_4$" apart.
3. Make plastic templates of the small apple and small leaf (page 33). Place templates in the center of each square and trace around template edges with light pencil lines.
4. Layer the batting on the remaining 12" x 15" piece of muslin.
5. Place the gridded muslin on top of the batting with the right side facing up.
6. Stitch all of the grid lines with black #8 perle cotton, using the running stitch. (See page 10.)

7. Stitch outlines of the apples and leaves with red and green #8 perle cotton. For the stems, make 2 long stitches with black perle cotton at the top of the apple next to the leaf.

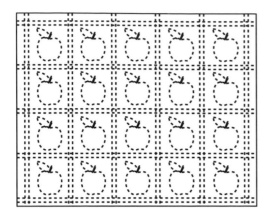

Appliquilt

Use templates on page 33.

1. Make plastic templates for the pie crust, pie dish, large apple, and large leaf, following the directions on page 9.

2. From the red scraps of fabric, cut 2 apples, and from the green, cut 2 leaves. From the blue, cut 1 pie dish, and from the tan checked fabric, cut 1 pie crust. Cut the pie top from the tea-dyed muslin.

3. Stitch the pieces to the gridded background, using contrasting colors of perle cotton. Stitch them in the order indicated by the numbered templates, following the directions on page 10. Refer to the quilt plan for placement.

4. Make a plastic template of the pie vent. Trace 3 vents onto the pie top, referring to the quilt plan for their location. Outline the vents with black perle cotton, using a running stitch.

Finishing

1. Sew the apple button to the pie top, following the directions on page 12.

2. Bind the edges with 1½"-wide strips of the blue checked fabric, following directions on page 11.

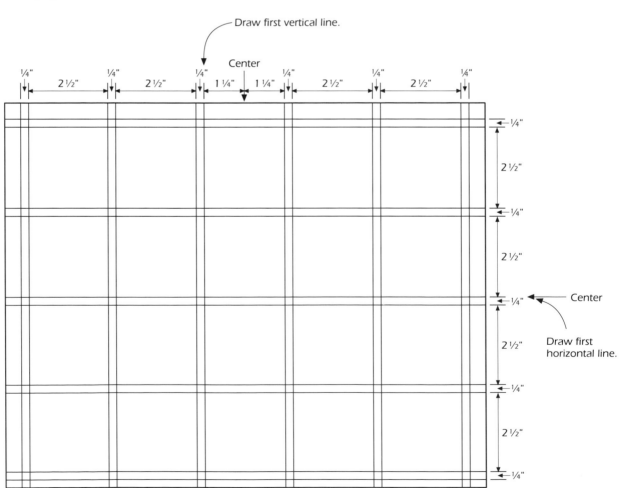

Grid Diagram

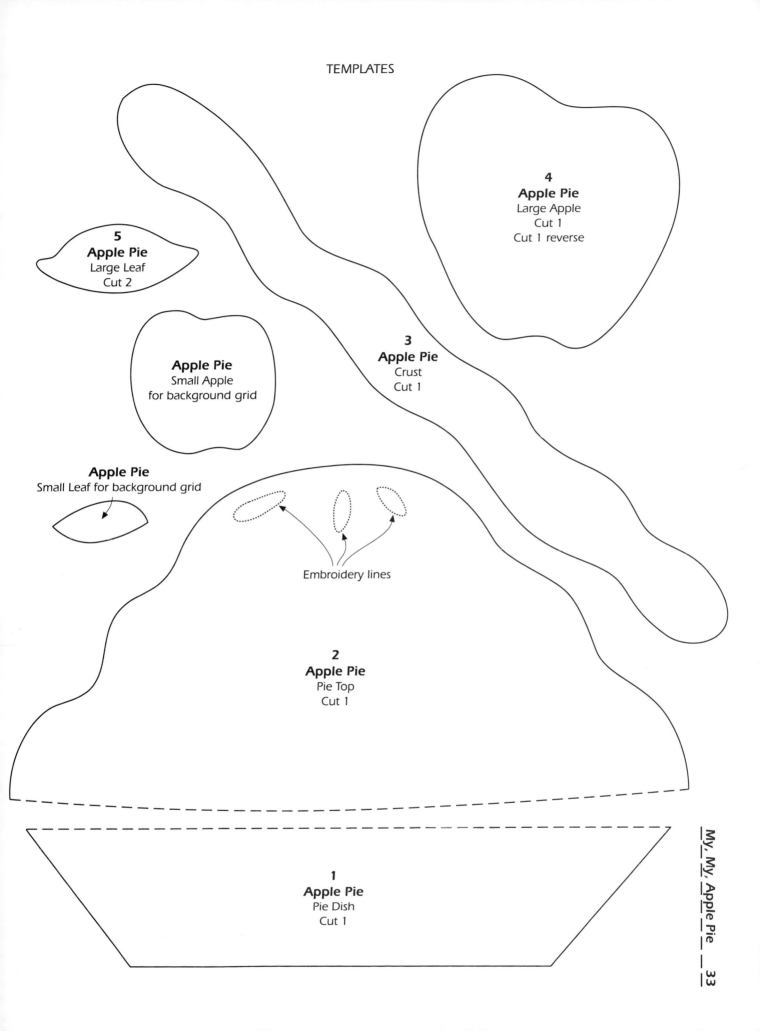

5
Apple Pie
Large Leaf
Cut 2

4
Apple Pie
Large Apple
Cut 1
Cut 1 reverse

Apple Pie
Small Apple
for background grid

3
Apple Pie
Crust
Cut 1

Apple Pie
Small Leaf for background grid

Embroidery lines

2
Apple Pie
Pie Top
Cut 1

1
Apple Pie
Pie Dish
Cut 1

Bunnies and Carrots

The bunnies and carrots would love to adorn your tabletop or brighten the wall in baby's room. Use up some of those scraps that you've been collecting.

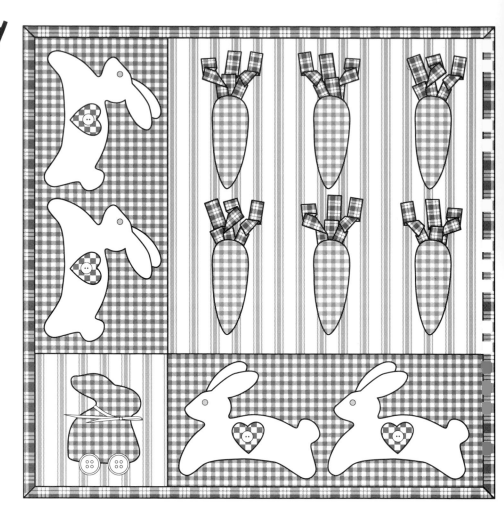

Color Photo: page 18
Size: 22" x 22"
Materials: 44"-wide fabric

1/2 yd. ticking or striped fabric for Carrots block and Bunny Pull-toy block

1/4 yd. blue checked (tiny checks) fabric for Leaping Bunnies block and Bunny Pull-toy block

Scraps: muslin for bunnies
    orange for carrots and hearts
    green for carrot tops

26" x 26" piece of fabric for backing

1/8 yd. blue plaid or fabric scraps for binding

26" x 26" piece of Pellon fleece or other thin batting

4 pink or white buttons for leaping bunnies' hearts

2 wood buttons for "wheels" on the bunny pull-toy

1 carrot button or charm for the bunny pull-toy

12" piece of 1/8"-wide orange ribbon

#8 perle cotton in assorted colors

Making the Foundation
Cutting
All seam allowances are 1/4" wide.

From the ticking, cut:
    1 square, 14 1/2" x 14 1/2", for Carrots block background
    1 square, 6 1/2" x 6 1/2", for Bunny Pull-toy block background

From the blue checked fabric, cut:
    2 rectangles, each 6 1/2" x 14 1/2", for Leaping Bunnies' block backgrounds

Directions
1. Layer the batting on the backing. See "Making the Quilt Sandwich Foundation" on page 8.
2. Place the 14 1/2" ticking square on the upper right corner of the batting, 2" down from the top and 2" in from the right side.

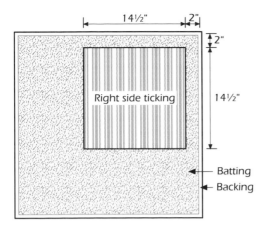

3. Matching the 14½" sides, place one of the 6½" x 14½" blue checked rectangles on the left side of the ticking square, right sides together. Pin in place. Machine stitch through all the layers.

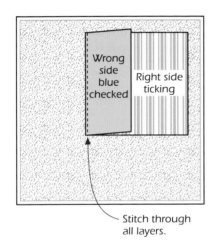

4. Flip the rectangle onto the batting. Press.

5. With right sides together, stitch the 6½" ticking square to the left side of the remaining 6½" x 14½" blue checked rectangle. Press the seam toward the ticking side.
6. Stitch the resulting unit to the bottom of the pieces that you have already sewn to the batting and backing. Match the seams at the corner where all 4 pieces intersect.

7. Flip this unit open onto the batting. Press. Your completed foundation should look like the illustration below.

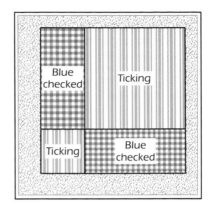

Appliquilt

Use templates on page 36.

1. Make plastic templates for the leaping bunny, bunny pull-toy, carrot, and heart, following the directions on page 9.
2. From the blue checked fabric, cut 1 bunny pull-toy. From the muslin, cut 4 leaping bunnies. From the orange, cut 6 carrots and 4 hearts. From the green, cut 18 strips, each ¼" wide, in lengths varying from 2½" to 5" long for the carrot tops.

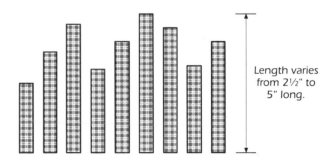

Make 18 strips, each ¼" wide.

3. Pin the ends of the green carrot-top strips in groups of 3 on the quilt. Refer to the Quilt Plan for placement. Sew them to the quilt with a short row of stitches.
4. Position the carrots on the carrot tops to just cover the stitching line that attached the carrot tops to the quilt. Stitch the carrots in place, following the directions on page 10.
5. Pin the leaping bunnies on the blue checked rectangles. Position the separate bunny ears slightly above the other ear (that is part of the template) and stitch. Stitch the leaping bunnies in place.

6. Stitch the small hearts to the centers of the leaping bunnies. The heart placement is shown on the template.

7. Before stitching the bunny pull-toy, place the ribbon behind the piece. Attach the ribbon to the quilt with 2 small stitches, then sew the pull-toy in place. Tie the ribbon into a bow around the bunny's neck.

Embellishments and Finishing

Refer to the Quilt Plan on page 34 for placement of buttons and eyes.

1. Sew the pink or white buttons to the centers of the hearts as shown on page 12.
2. Attach a carrot button if desired.
3. Sew the wood-look buttons to the bottom of the pull-toy for wheels.
4. Make French knots for the bunnies' eyes.
5. If you don't like the look of the carrot tops flopping down, secure them to the quilt by making a single stitch at the top and in the middle of each strip. Tie each stitch with a double knot.
6. Bind the edges with 1¼"-wide strips of blue plaid, following the directions on page 11.

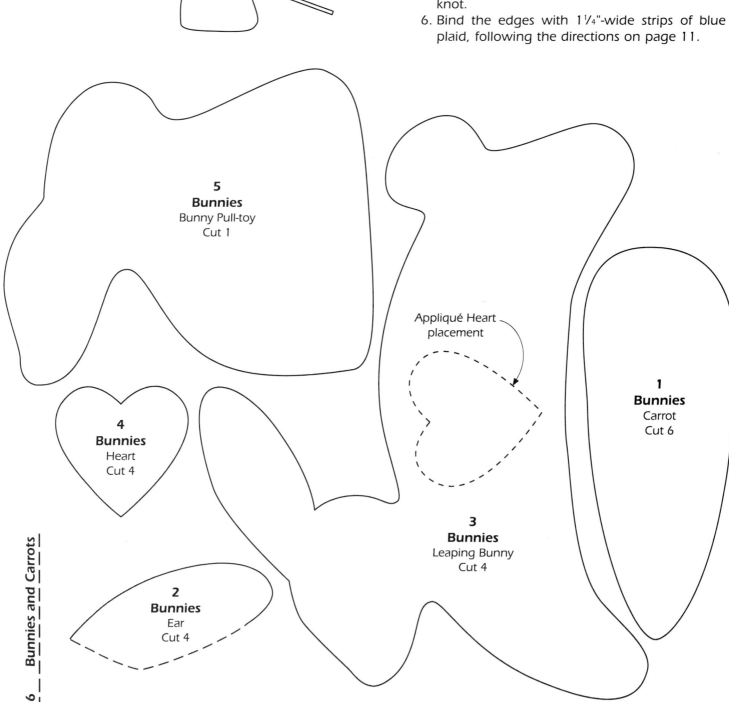

Sew ribbon under bunny before stitching bunny in place.

5
Bunnies
Bunny Pull-toy
Cut 1

Appliqué Heart placement

1
Bunnies
Carrot
Cut 6

4
Bunnies
Heart
Cut 4

3
Bunnies
Leaping Bunny
Cut 4

2
Bunnies
Ear
Cut 4

Hearts 'n' Hands

Pastel floral fabrics and small golden charms would give this design a Victorian flair, or try bright primary colors for a totally different look. Experiment and have fun with this one!

Color Photo: page 19
Size: 28" x 28"
Materials: 44"-wide fabric

½ yd. total of 5 different blue plaids and prints for Heart blocks, Hand blocks, hearts, and Log Cabin blocks

¼ yd. each of 2 different blues or fabric scraps for outer border

⅛ yd. each of 5 different yellows for Log Cabin blocks, hearts, and inner border

1 yd. muslin for hands and backing

¼ yd. blue-and-yellow print for hearts and binding

34" x 34" piece of Pellon fleece or other thin batting

#8 perle cotton in assorted colors

Assorted blue, yellow, and white buttons

Making the Foundation
Cutting
All seam allowances are ¼" wide.

For the Heart and Hand blocks, cut:
  4 rectangles, each 5½" x 10½", from 1 blue for Hand backgrounds
  2 rectangles, each 5½" x 15½", from 2 different blues for Heart backgrounds

For the Log Cabin blocks, cut:
  2 squares, each 1½" x 1½", from one blue for centers
  2 squares, each 1½" x 1½", from 2 different blues
  2 strips, each 1½" x 2½", from the third blue
  2 strips, each 1½" x 3½", from the fourth blue
  2 strips, each 1½" x 4½", from the fifth blue
  2 strips, each 1½" x 2½", from the first yellow
  2 strips, each 1½" x 3½", from the second yellow
  2 strips, each 1½" x 4½", from the third yellow
  2 strips, each 1½" x 5½", from the fourth yellow

For the inner border strips, cut:

1 strip, 2" x 20½", from the first yellow for left border

2 strips, each 2" x 22", from the first and second yellows for top and right borders

1 strip, 2" x 23½", from the second yellow for bottom border

For the outer border strips, cut:

1 strip, 3" x 23½", from the first blue for left border

2 strips, each 3" x 26", from the first and second blues for top and right borders

1 strip, 3" x 28½", from the second blue for bottom border

From the muslin, cut:

1 square, 32" x 32", for backing

Directions

1. Layer the batting on the backing. See "Making the Quilt Sandwich Foundation" on page 8.
2. Make 2 Log Cabin blocks. For each block:
   a. Stitch a 1½" x 1½" blue center square to a different blue 1½" x 1½" square. Finger press the seam.
   b. Stitch a blue strip, 1½" x 2½", to the bottom of the unit made in the step above. Finger press the seam.

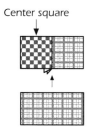

Center square

c. Add the remaining strips in a clockwise direction as shown.

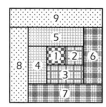

Log Cabin Block
Make 2.

   d. Press both blocks. Measure and trim if necessary to make them 5½" x 5½" squares.

3. Matching the 5½" sides, sew a yellow side of a Log Cabin block to a 5½" x 10½" blue rectangle. Press. Make 2. Label Unit #1.

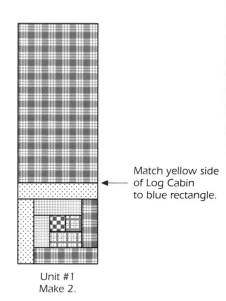

Match yellow side of Log Cabin to blue rectangle.

Unit #1
Make 2.

4. Sew Unit #1 to a long side of a 5½" x 15½" blue rectangle. Press. Make 2. Label Unit #2.

Unit #1

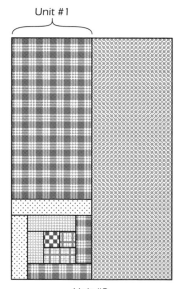

Unit #2
Make 2.

5. Sew Unit #2 to the 10½" side of a 5½" x 10½" blue rectangle. Press. Make 2. Label Unit #3. This completes construction of both halves of the quilt-top background.

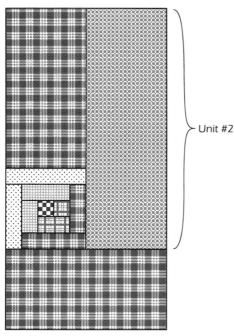

Unit #3
Make 2.

6. With a pencil or fabric marker, draw lines through the center of the batting both vertically and horizontally.

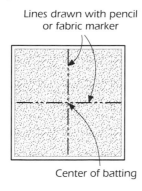

Lines drawn with pencil or fabric marker

Center of batting

7. Place the two quilt-top halves (Unit #3) next to each other as shown. The one on the left side is Unit #3a and the one on the right is Unit #3b.

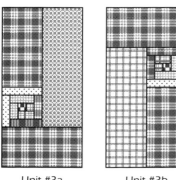

Unit #3a   Unit #3b

8. Place Unit #3b on top of Unit #3a with right sides together. Use a pencil or fabric marker to draw a ¼"-wide seam allowance along the right edge. Lay the quilt-top halves (with right sides together) on the batting, aligning the seam line with the vertical center line and placing it 6" below the top edge of the batting.

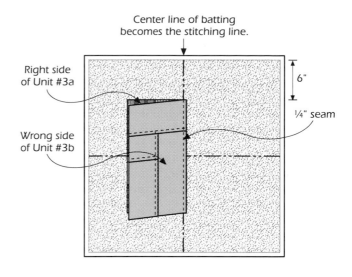

Center line of batting becomes the stitching line.

Right side of Unit #3a

Wrong side of Unit #3b

6"

¼" seam

9. Machine stitch the quilt-top halves to the batting and backing on the seam line, which is also the center line of the batting. Flip Unit #3b onto the batting. Press.

10. Pin-baste the top and bottom edges of Units #3a and #3b to the batting and backing, following the directions on page 8.

11. Machine or hand quilt in-the-ditch around the center quilt blocks. Leave the pins in place.

12. Add the borders. Place the yellow left inner border strip on the left side of the quilt top. With right sides together, stitch through all of the layers.

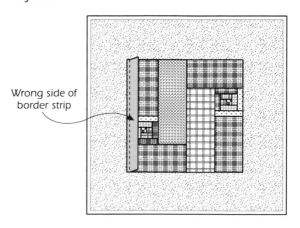

Wrong side of border strip

13. Flip the border onto the batting. Press.

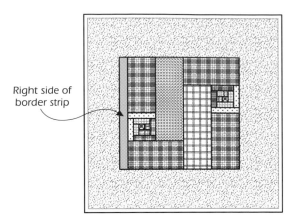

Right side of border strip

14. Repeat the same procedure with the top, right, and bottom inner borders, in that order, pressing the seam after each border is added.

15. Following the same procedure, add the blue outer borders, starting with the left border, then the top, right, and bottom borders. Refer to the quilt plan to see how your completed foundation should look.

Appliquilt

Use templates on pages 40-41.

1. Make plastic templates for the hearts and hands, following the directions on page 9.
2. Cut the pieces from the fabrics noted in the "Materials" list.
3. Referring to the quilt plan for placement, stitch the hands and the large hearts in place first, then stitch the smaller hearts on top of them as indicated on the templates. I placed contrasting fabrics on top of each other and stitched with contrasting colors of perle cotton.

Embellishments and Finishing

1. Quilt around the strips in the Log Cabin blocks, just inside the seam lines, with perle cotton, using a running stitch. See page 10. Quilt around the yellow border strip just inside both seam lines.
2. Using the quilting pattern on page 41 and a quilt marker, trace the quilting pattern onto the 2½"-wide outer border. Quilt with perle cotton in a contrasting color, sewing the buttons onto the border as you go. See the directions for attaching buttons on page 12.
3. Sew buttons to the centers of the Log Cabin block, hearts, and hands. For an added touch, I placed a 1" x 1" square of contrasting fabric under each button on the medium-sized hearts before attaching the buttons.
4. Bind the edges with 1¼"-wide strips of the blue-and-yellow print, following the directions on page 11.

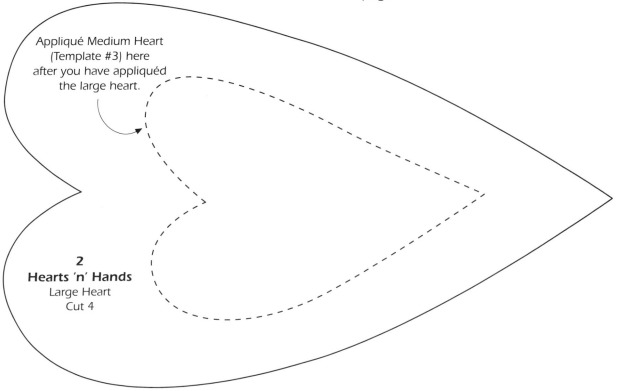

Appliqué Medium Heart
(Template #3) here
after you have appliquéd
the large heart.

2
Hearts 'n' Hands
Large Heart
Cut 4

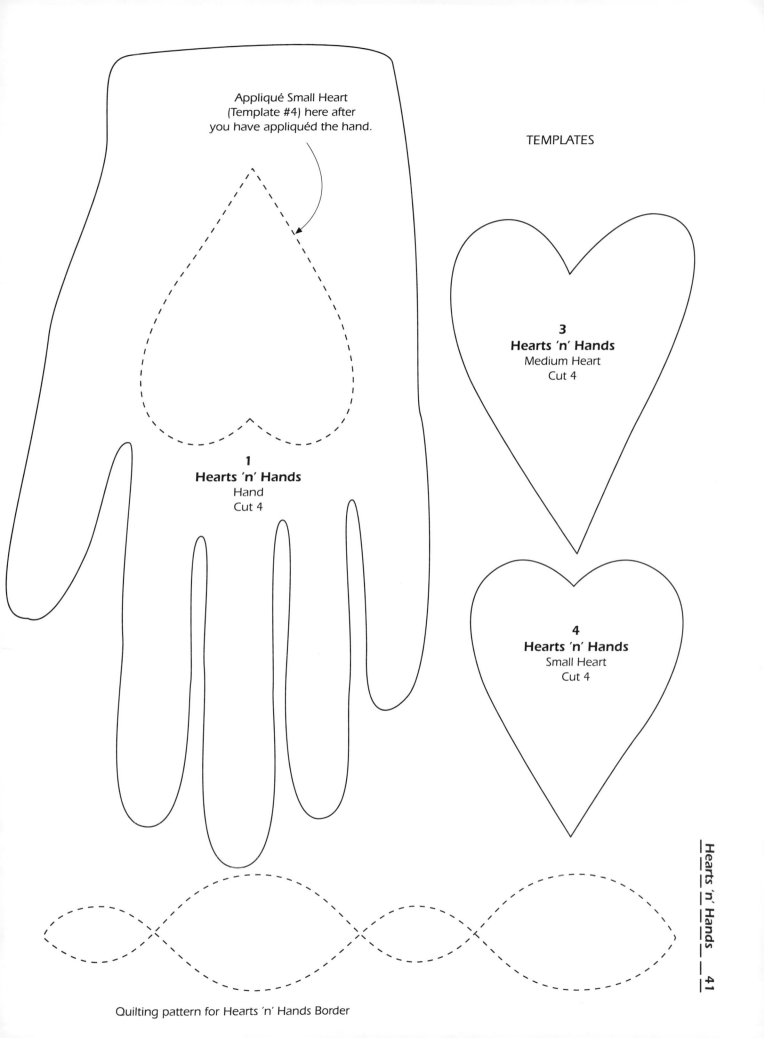

Appliqué Small Heart
(Template #4) here after
you have appliquéd the hand.

TEMPLATES

1
Hearts 'n' Hands
Hand
Cut 4

3
Hearts 'n' Hands
Medium Heart
Cut 4

4
Hearts 'n' Hands
Small Heart
Cut 4

Quilting pattern for Hearts 'n' Hands Border

Animal Stack

I've been told that an animal stack is a symbol of good luck. I hope this is true—you decide! This design brings the country right into your home.

Color Photo: page 21
Size: 26" x 36"
Materials: 44"-wide fabric

¾ yd. ticking for background, checkerboard, and binding

⅜ yd. dark plaid for checkerboard and borders

⅜ yd. tea-dyed cow print (See the tea-dyeing recipe on page 6.)

Scraps: White-and-gray striped fabric for sheep
Peach for pig, cow's udder, and muzzle
White with black dots (tea-dyed) for chicken
Red orange for chicken wattle and comb
Tea-dyed muslin for feed bag
Dark plaids for Four Patch Squares
Black for cow-head shadow

30" x 40" piece of fabric for backing

30" x 40" piece of Pellon fleece or other thin batting

#8 perle cotton in assorted colors

Jute

Black permanent marker

Assorted buttons

Small cow bells and hay bales

Tracing paper (optional)

Transfer pen or pencil (optional)

Making the Foundation

Cutting

All seams are ¼" wide.

From the ticking, cut:
- 1 rectangle, 20½" x 26½", for background
- 1 strip, 2½" x 25", for checkerboard

From the dark plaid, cut:
- 1 strip, 2½" x 25", for checkerboard
- 2 strips, each 3½" x 26½", for top and bottom borders
- 2 strips, each 3½" x 30½", for side borders

Directions

1. With right sides together, stitch the 2½" x 25" ticking and plaid strips together along one long edge. Press the seam to one side.
2. Crosscut the sewn strip into ten 2½"-wide segments as shown.

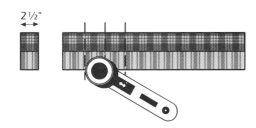

3. Stitch the 2½"-wide pieces together, alternating the position of the plaid square and striped squares as shown to make a checkerboard-patterned block.

4. With right sides together, sew the checkerboard to one end of the 20½" x 26½" ticking rectangle. This completes the quilt top background.

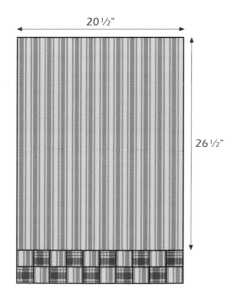

5. Layer the batting between the quilt-top background and the backing. Position the quilt top so that it is in the center of the batting with 4" of backing extending beyond the edges of the top. Pin-baste the layers together. See "Making the Quilt Sandwich Foundation" on page 8.
6. Machine or hand quilt in-the-ditch between the checkerboard block and the ticking block/background.
7. Add the side borders. With right sides together, stitch through all the layers.

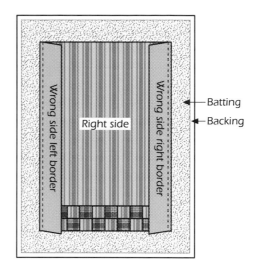

8. Flip the borders over the batting. Press. Repeat this procedure to add the top and bottom borders. Your completed foundation should look like the illustration below.

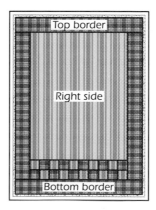

Appliquilt

Use templates on pages 45–48.

1. Make plastic templates for the animals, following the directions on page 9.
2. Cut the pieces from the fabrics noted in the "Materials" list.

3. You are now ready to stitch the animals in place. See Appliquilting directions on page 10 and refer to the quilt plan for placement of the pieces. Stitch the animals with perle cotton in the order indicated by the numbered templates. Special instructions follow for the pig and cow.

a. For the pig's tail, cut a ¼" x 2½" strip from the peach fabric. Stitch it to the quilt top, before stitching the pig.

b. For the cow, first stitch the body (Template #12) in place. Layer the black head piece behind the cow-print head (both cut from Template #13), offsetting the black behind the cow print as shown. This helps to outline the cow's head and define the body.

Offset black fabric cow head behind cow print.

Pin the head in place on the body. Thread a 2½" piece of jute through the cow bell and attach the jute to the quilt under the cow head with 2 small stitches. Be sure the bell hangs below the cow head. Stitch the cow head over the top of the jute. Next, stitch the muzzle and the udder in place.

Embellishments

Feed Sack

1. Cut a 2½" x 5" piece of tea-dyed muslin. Cut two 3"-long pieces of jute. Crimp 2 corners of the muslin piece and tie with the jute.

Tie corners with jute.

2. Using a black permanent marker, write "FEED" on feed sack, or you may wish to transfer the word "FEED" from page 45. To do this, use a transfer pen or pencil to trace the letters onto a sheet of tracing paper. Hold the paper up to a window or other light source and trace in reverse on the opposite side. Iron these reversed letters onto the right side of the muslin piece, following the manufacturer's directions. Finally, go over the transferred letters with a black permanent marker.

3. Stitch the feed sack to the top of the quilt with a contrasting color of perle cotton.

Four Patch Squares

1. Cut 1 strip, 1½" x 15", from each of 2 different dark plaids. With right sides together, stitch the 2 strips together along one long edge. Press seam to one side. As you did with the checkerboard, cut the strip into 1½"-wide pieces.

2. Sew 2 of these pieces together so that like plaids are diagonally opposite each other as shown. Make 5 Four Patch squares. Trim the edges with pinking shears and stitch them to the top, referring to the quilt plan for their placement.

Make 5.

3. Sew buttons in the centers of the Four Patch squares. Directions for attaching buttons are on page 12.

Checkerboard

1. Quilt the striped 2" x 2" squares of the checkerboard twice diagonally through the centers as shown, using a contrasting color of perle cotton.

2. Sew buttons in the centers of the 2" x 2" plaid squares of the checkerboard.

Hay Bales

1. With epoxy glue, attach a hay bale to each end of an 8"-long piece of jute. Allow to dry thoroughly. Make a loop with the jute and machine stitch it to the quilt where the jute crosses.

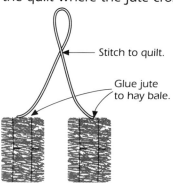

Stitch to quilt.

Glue jute to hay bale.

2. Sew a button over the area of the jute that you machine stitched.

Finishing

Bind the edges with 1½"-wide strips of the dark plaid, following the directions on page 11.

TEMPLATES

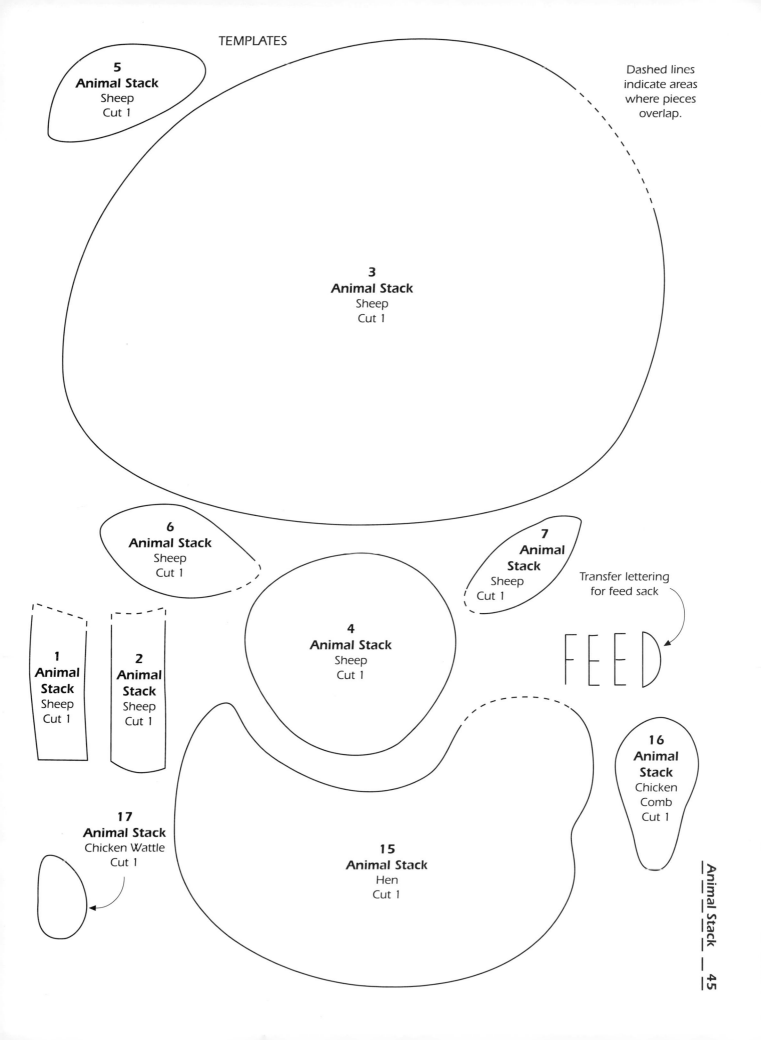

5
Animal Stack
Sheep
Cut 1

3
Animal Stack
Sheep
Cut 1

Dashed lines
indicate areas
where pieces
overlap.

6
Animal Stack
Sheep
Cut 1

7
Animal Stack
Sheep
Cut 1

Transfer lettering
for feed sack

FEED

1
Animal Stack
Sheep
Cut 1

2
Animal Stack
Sheep
Cut 1

4
Animal Stack
Sheep
Cut 1

16
Animal Stack
Chicken
Comb
Cut 1

17
Animal Stack
Chicken Wattle
Cut 1

15
Animal Stack
Hen
Cut 1

Animal Stack — 45

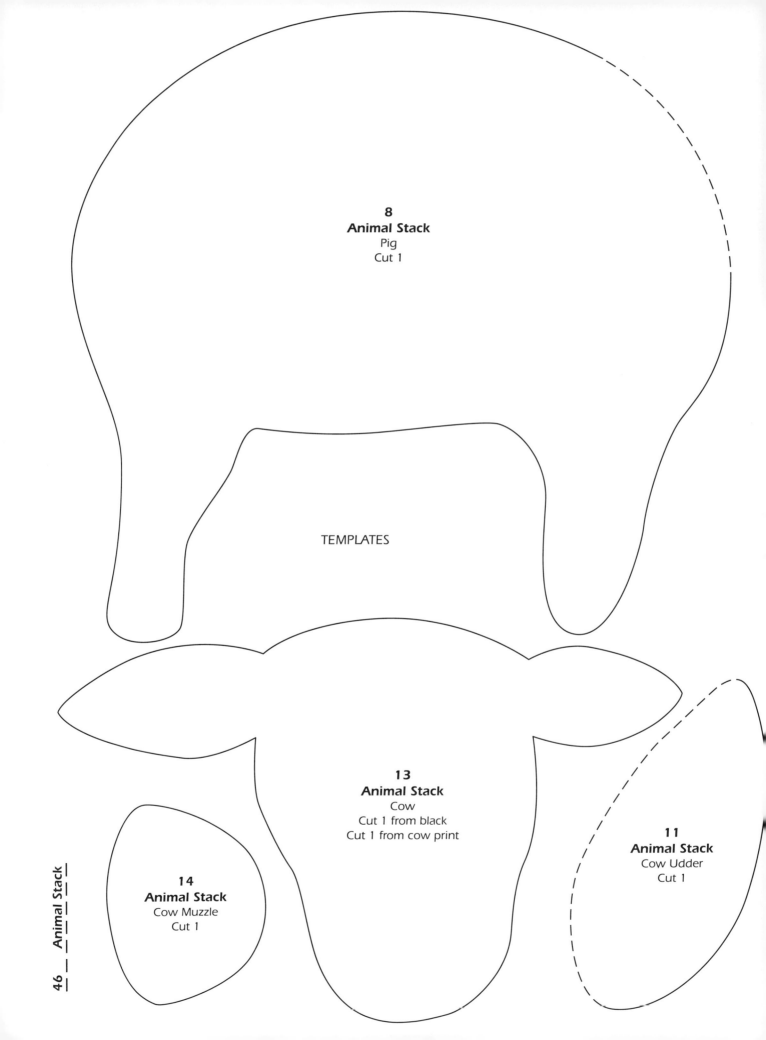

8
Animal Stack
Pig
Cut 1

TEMPLATES

13
Animal Stack
Cow
Cut 1 from black
Cut 1 from cow print

11
Animal Stack
Cow Udder
Cut 1

14
Animal Stack
Cow Muzzle
Cut 1

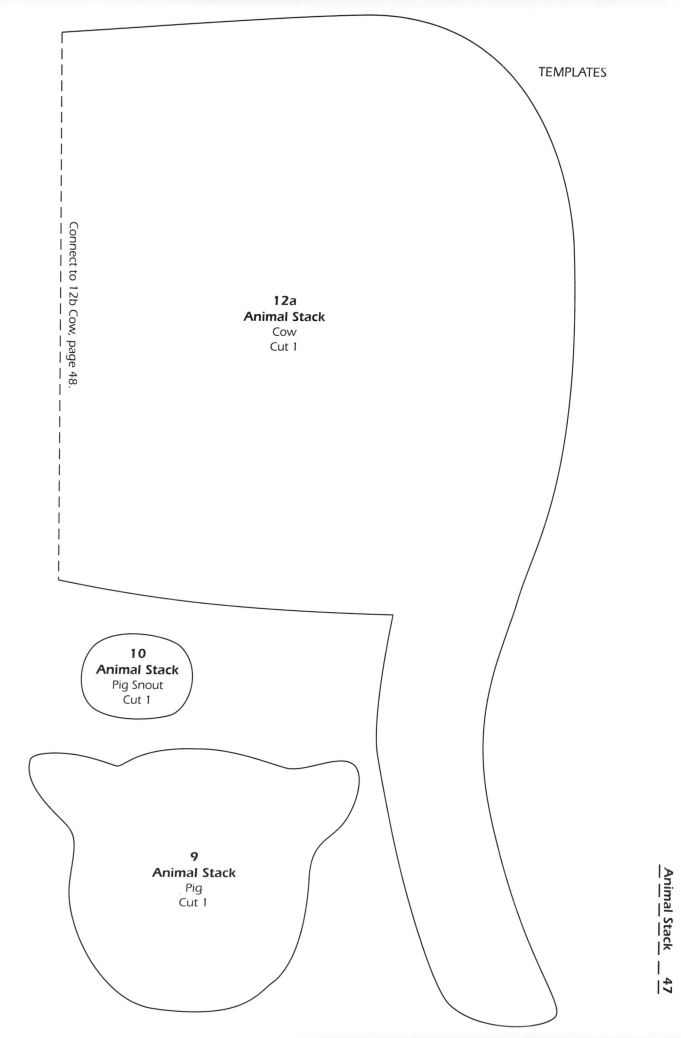

Connect to 12b Cow, page 48.

12a
Animal Stack
Cow
Cut 1

10
Animal Stack
Pig Snout
Cut 1

9
Animal Stack
Pig
Cut 1

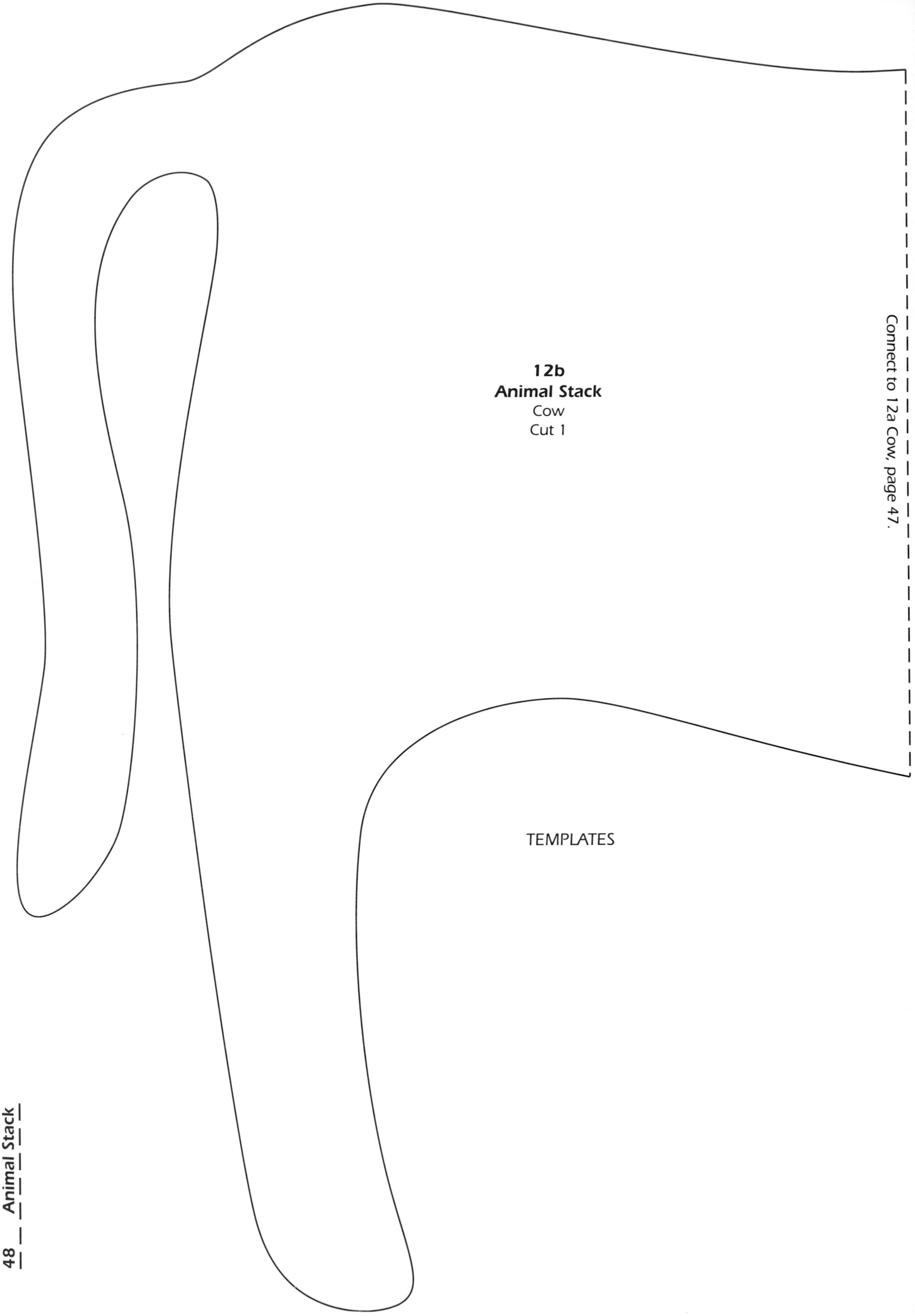

12b
Animal Stack
Cow
Cut 1

Connect to 12a Cow, page 47.

TEMPLATES

God Bless America

Here's a chance for you to make a wonderful Americana-style quilt to show your love of country and have a geography lesson at the same time. To personalize it, add a golden star to locate the capital in your home state.

Color Photo: page 23
Size: 28" x 38"
Materials: 44"-wide fabric

1³⁄₈ yds. dark star print for stars, background, corners in the border, and binding

½ yd. red-and-white striped fabric for border

¼ yd. tan background star fabric for stars

½ yd. tea-dyed muslin for the U.S. map (See tea-dyeing recipe on page 6.)

Scraps: 2 browns for dog
   Flesh color for girl
   2 contrasting fabrics for dress and apron

32" x 42" piece of fabric for backing

32" x 42" piece of Pellon fleece or other thin batting

#8 perle cotton in assorted colors, including navy blue

Jute

Wool (3-ply) for lettering

24 assorted buttons for centers of each star

Small red beads to mark the location of the state capital

4 medium-sized black buttons for girl's hair

American flag (approximately 3" x 4")

Tracing paper (optional)

Transfer pen or pencil (optional)

Making the Foundation
Cutting

All seams are ¼" wide.
Use the map transfer pattern on the
pullout pattern insert.

From the dark star print, cut:
 1 rectangle, 20½" x 30½", for map background
 4 squares, each 4½" x 4½", for border corner squares

From the red-and-white striped fabric, cut:
 2 strips, each 4½" x 20½", for side borders
 2 strips, each 4½" x 30½", for top and bottom borders

Directions

1. Layer the batting on the backing. See "Making the Quilt Sandwich Foundation" on page 8.
2. Place the 20½" x 30½" map background rectangle in the center of the batting.
3. With right sides together, pin and sew the top and bottom border strips to the top and bottom edges of the background rectangle, stitching through all the layers.

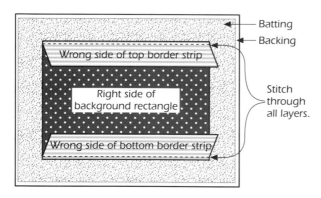

4. Flip the border strips right side up onto the batting. Press.

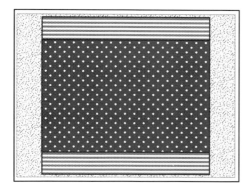

5. To make the side borders, sew the 4½" x 4½" squares to both ends of each remaining border strip. Press the seam toward the dark side.

Make 2.

6. Sew side borders to the background, right sides together, through all the layers as you did with the top and bottom borders. Press. Your completed foundation should look like the illustration below.

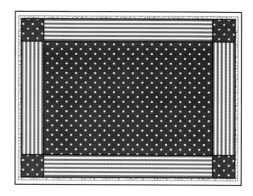

7. Trace over all of the lines on the map transfer pattern with a transfer pen. (If you do not have a transfer pen, use a light table or tape the pattern to a window and trace the lines onto the muslin with a pencil.)
8. Carefully center and pin the traced pattern onto the piece of tea-dyed muslin.
9. Press the design onto the muslin, following the manufacturer's directions. To be sure that your lines are transferring onto the fabric, occasionally lift the paper very carefully. Check your lines and replace the paper pattern on the fabric in the same position. It is important not to shift your paper pattern at all during this step or you will have double lines. These lines are permanent.
10. After the map pattern has been transferred, cut ¼" outside the outline, using pinking shears. Position the map on the background.
11. Use the same method to transfer the words "God Bless America." Go over all writing with your transfer pen. Cut the words apart and place, written side down, on the background. Position the words and the map before you appliquilt to ensure proper placement.

Appliquilt

Use templates on the pullout pattern insert.

1. Make plastic templates for the girl, her dress and apron, the dog, and the stars, following the directions on page 9.
2. From the fabrics noted in the "Materials" list, cut out the girl, her dress and apron, and the dog. From the dark star print, cut 20 stars. From the tan background star fabric, cut 4 stars.
3. Stitch the map onto the background, following the directions on page 10. Stitch all lines on the map, using navy blue perle cotton.
4. With the map stitched in place, pin the girl, flag, and dog in place. Refer to the quilt plan for their location. Next, lay the jute in place, running it under the girl's hand, under the top of the flag, and between the dog's head and body. You may either tack down the jute by hand, using the couching method, or machine stitch it to the background, using a zigzag stitch and invisible thread.

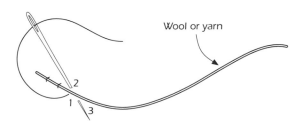

Couching by Hand

Stitch the girl, dog, and flag to the map with perle cotton in the order indicated by the numbered templates.
5. Stitch the stars in place on the borders.

Embellishments and Finishing

1. Stitch a button to the center of each star, following directions for attaching buttons on page 12.
2. Place the 3-ply wool on top of the "God Bless America" lettering that was previously transferred onto the fabric. With thread to match the wool, make tiny stitches at ½"–¾" intervals by bringing the thread up from the bottom of the quilt to the top and then over the wool and back down to the back of the quilt. Stitch in a continuous line until all letters have been couched with wool.
3. Attach small, red beads to the map, referring to the dots on the map pattern for placement. These represent the state capitals. You may want to denote areas where you have lived or visited or where friends and relatives live instead of the

capitals. You may want to use a different colored bead for these places.
4. Make French knots (page 12) for the girl's eyes or use small beads.
5. Stitch black buttons in place for hair by bringing 2 strands of perle cotton through each button. Knot them together, trim away all but ½", and fray the ends as shown.

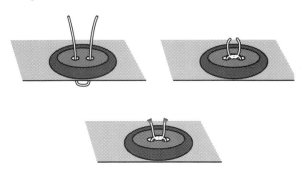

6. Bind the edges with 1½"-wide strips of the dark star print, following the directions on page 11.

Sunflowers and Crows

Sunflowers growing in rich brown soil, and crows basking in the warm sun are true signs of summer.

Color photo: page 20
Size: 30" x 40"
Materials: 44"-wide fabric

1 yd. black-and-white striped fabric for sky

¼ yd. brown-and-black checked fabric for ground

¼ yd. of a plaid fabric for left and top borders

⅛ yd. striped fabric for right border

¼ yd. of black-and-gray print for picket fence

⅜ yd. tea-dyed yellow gingham for sun (See the tea-dyeing recipe on page 6.)

Scraps: At least 4 different yellow/golds for sunflowers

    At least 3 different greens for leaves and stems

    At least 3 different dark fabrics for flower centers

    Black for crows

⅛ yd. black solid fabric for binding

34" x 44" piece of fabric for backing

34" x 44" piece of Pellon fleece or other thin batting

#8 perle cotton in assorted colors, including black

Ladybug buttons

Making the Foundation
Cutting
All seams are ¼" wide.

From the black-and-white striped fabric, cut:
  1 rectangle, 22½" x 35½", for the sky

From the brown-and-black checked fabric, cut:
  1 rectangle, 6½" x 35½", for the ground

From the plaid border fabric, cut:
  1 strip, 3½" x 28½", for the left border
  1 strip, 2½" x 38½", for the top border

From the striped border fabric, cut:
  1 strip, 2½" x 30½", for the right border

Directions

1. Layer the batting on the backing. See "Making the Quilt Sandwich Foundation" on page 8.
2. Place the sky rectangle, right side up, on top of the batting 5" below the top edge.
3. With right sides together, pin and stitch the ground rectangle to the bottom edge of the sky rectangle, stitching through all the layers.

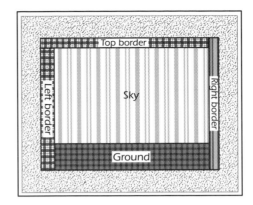

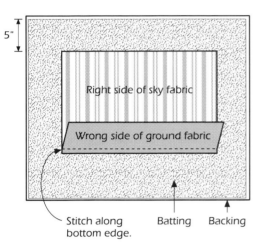

4. Flip the ground rectangle onto the batting. Press.
5. With right sides together, pin the left border strip to the left side of the sky and ground unit. Stitch through all the layers.

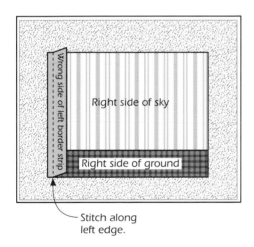

6. Flip the border onto the batting. Press.
7. With right sides together, pin the top border strip to the top edges of the foundation. Stitch through all the layers, as you did in the previous step. Flip the border onto the batting. Press.
8. Repeat the same process to add the right border to the foundation. Press. Your completed foundation should look like the illustration below.

9. Bind the edges with 1½"-wide strips of black fabric, following the directions on page 11.

Appliquilt

Use templates on pages 54–63.

1. Make plastic templates for the crows, sun and sun rays, picket fence, sunflowers, and leaves, following the directions on page 9. When making picket template #2, follow the instructions on the template to make it one piece. Template #6 is made in the same manner. Be sure to label your templates as you make them, for easy reference later.
2. Cut the pieces from the fabrics noted in the "Materials" list.
3. Referring to the quilt plan for placement, stitch the pieces in the order indicated by the numbered templates. See Appliquilting directions on page 10. Follow the additional steps below for the best results.

   a. **Picket fence** (Templates #1 through #11). Stitch the pickets in order from left to right across the quilt. Template #1 is the first picket on the left.

   b. **Flower stems** (Templates #12 through #20). Stitch the stems in order from left to right. Template #12 is the first one on the left. Colors listed on the templates are only suggestions. Choose your own colors if you wish.

   c. **Flowers** (Templates #21a and #21b through #26a and #26b). Stitch the flowers in the order of the template numbers and letters. For example, stitch #23a before #23b. In some cases, you stitch the flower centers first, then the petal portion. On other flowers, you stitch the petal portions first, then the centers. Be sure that you remove the centers from the fabric pieces that you cut, when using Templates #23b and #25b.

d. **Leaves** (Templates #27, #28, and #29). Stitch leaves in any order, referring to the quilt plan for their placement.

e. **Crows** (Template #30). From the black fabric, cut 1 crow with the template right side up on the right side of the fabric. Cut the other crow with the template wrong side up on the right side of the fabric.

f. **Sun** (Templates #31–#34). After stitching the sun rays in place, stitch the sun, overlapping the rays slightly.

Embellishments

1. To add texture to the ground, quilt 9 straight lines in the ground area with black perle cotton. Use a running stitch and vary the lengths of the lines from 5" to 8".

2. Sew ladybug buttons or other embellishments onto the quilt. Directions for sewing on buttons appear on page 12.

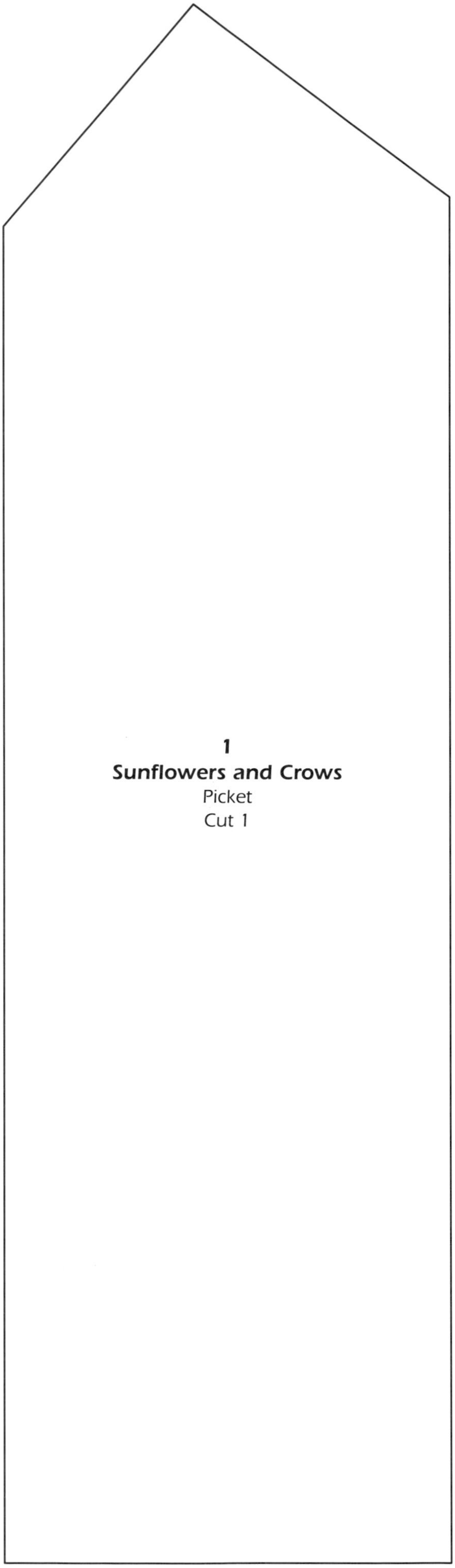

1
Sunflowers and Crows
Picket
Cut 1

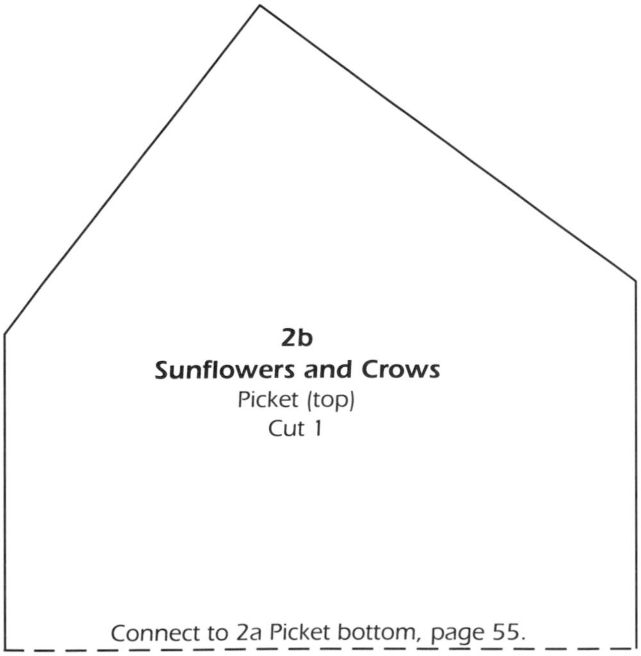

2b
Sunflowers and Crows
Picket (top)
Cut 1

Connect to 2a Picket bottom, page 55.

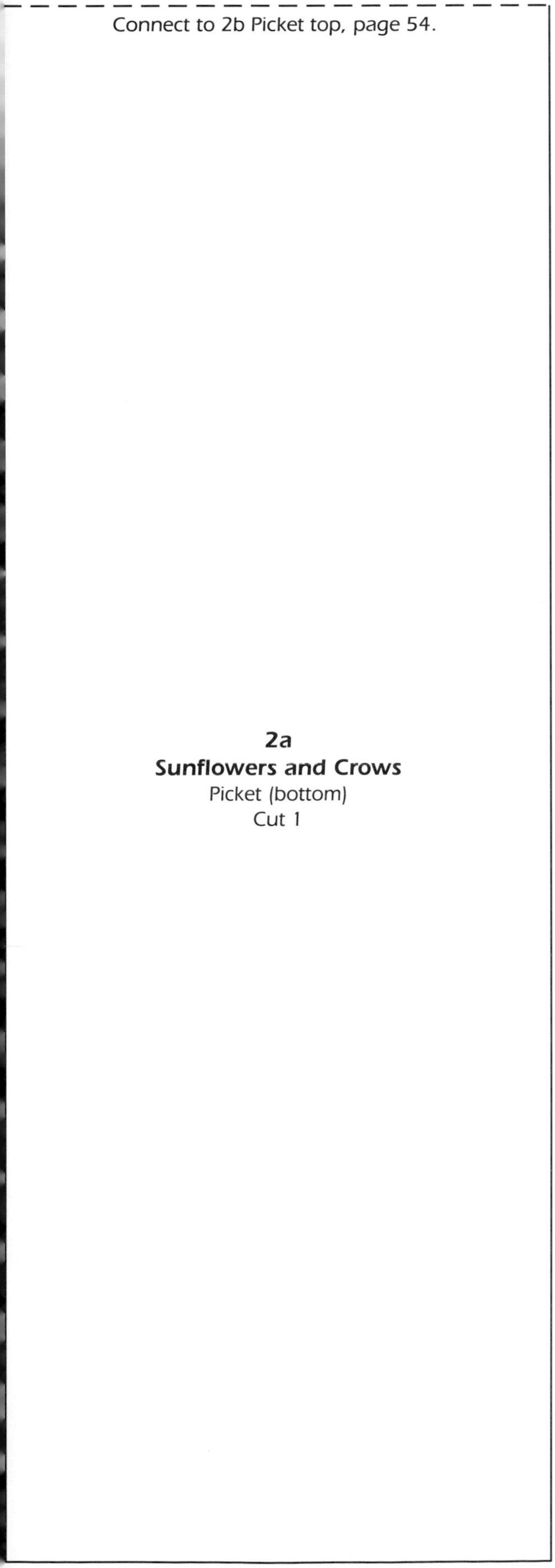

Connect to 2b Picket top, page 54.

2a
Sunflowers and Crows
Picket (bottom)
Cut 1

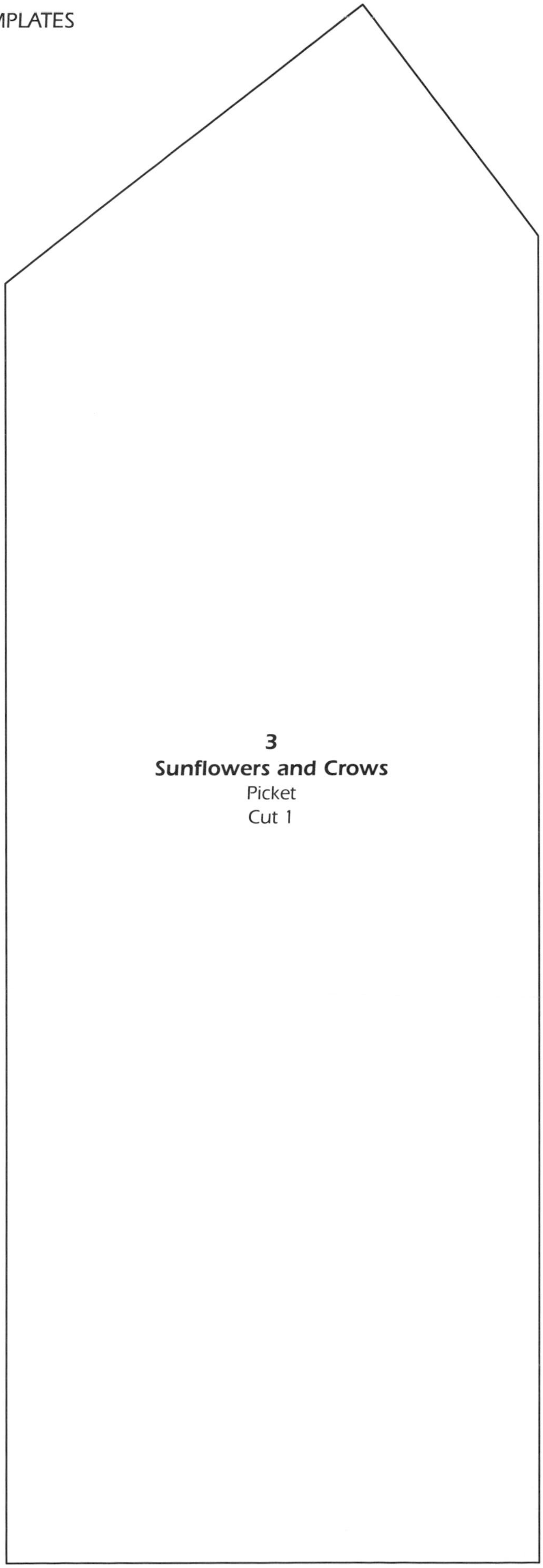

3
Sunflowers and Crows
Picket
Cut 1

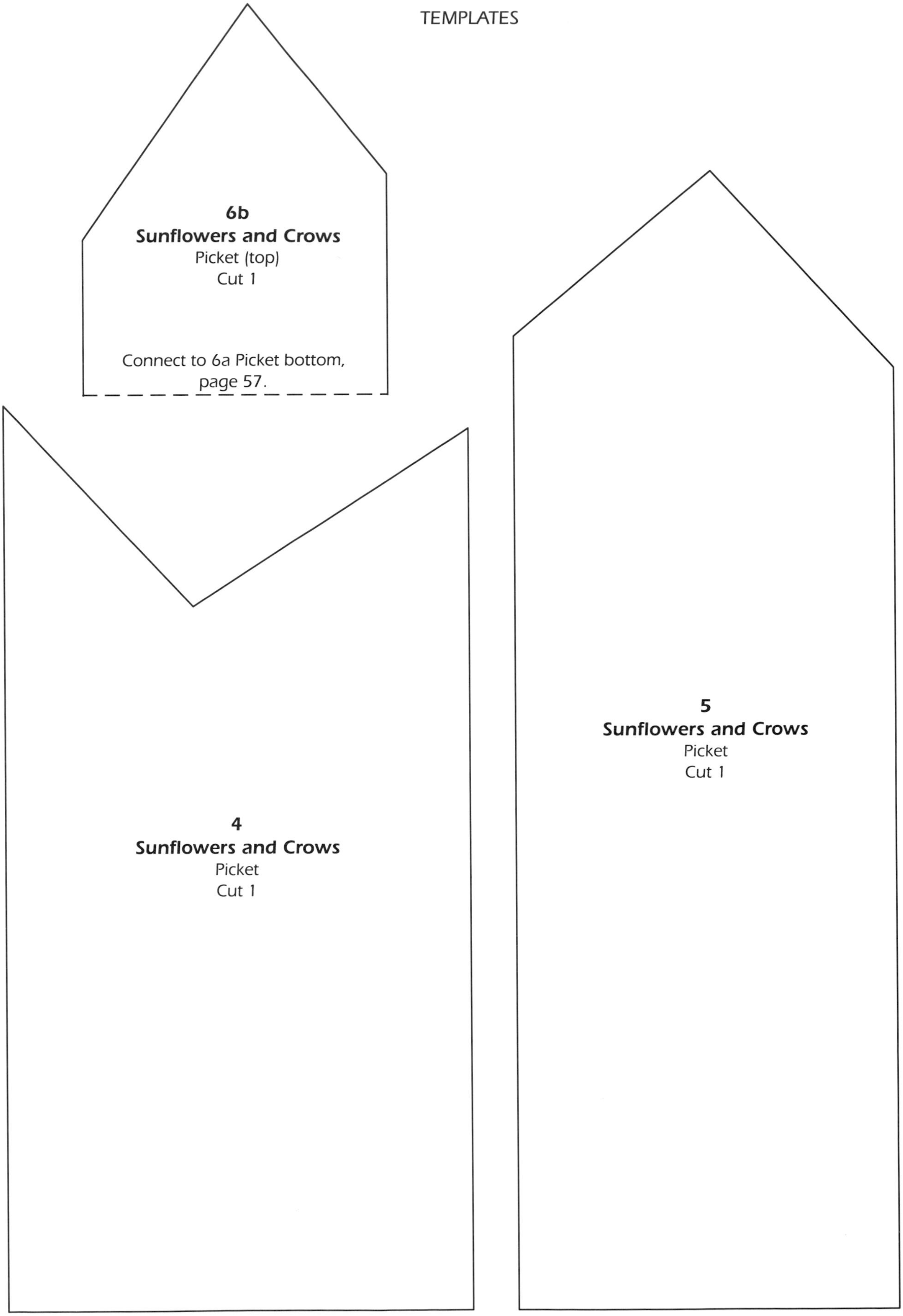

6b
Sunflowers and Crows
Picket (top)
Cut 1

Connect to 6a Picket bottom,
page 57.

5
Sunflowers and Crows
Picket
Cut 1

4
Sunflowers and Crows
Picket
Cut 1

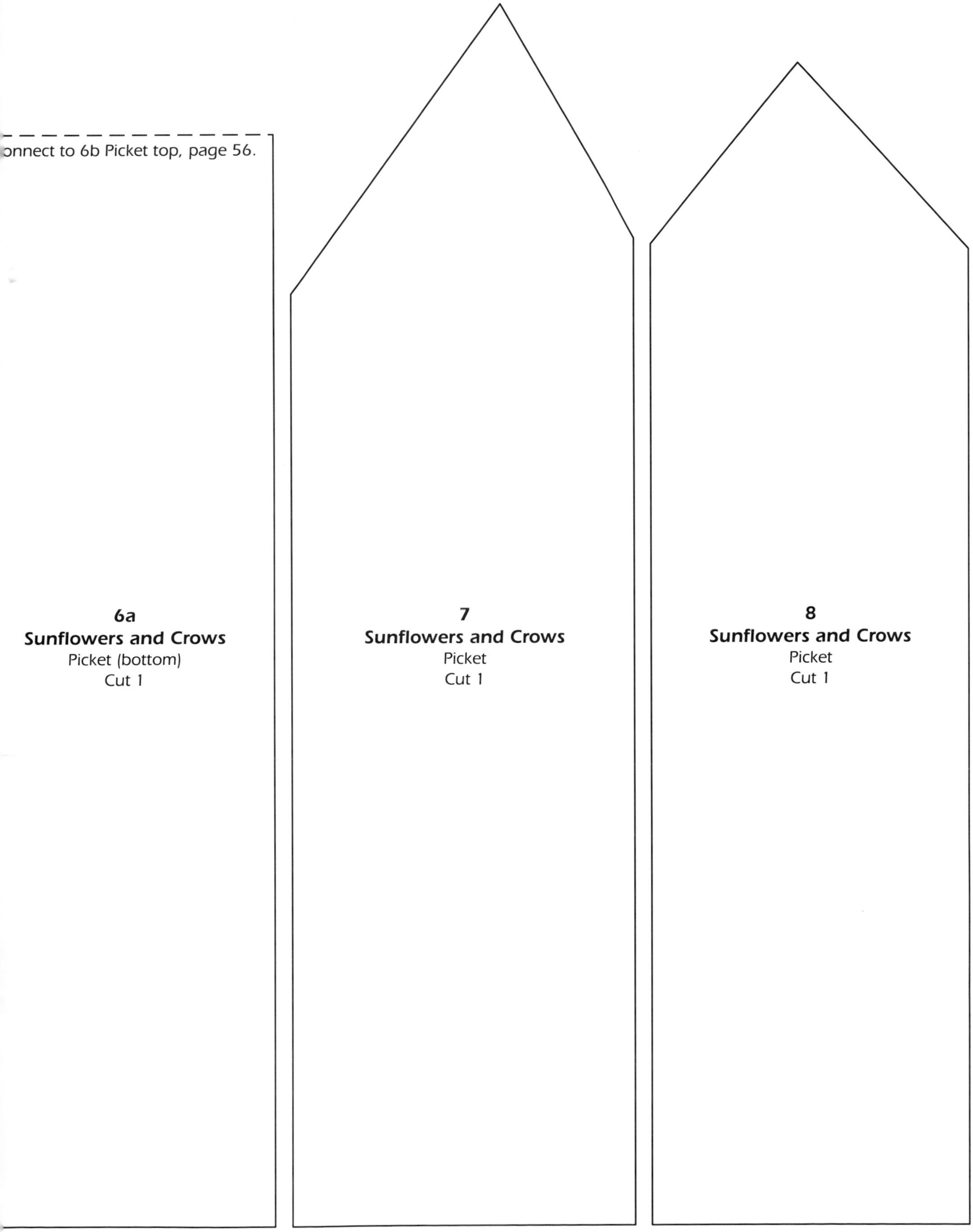

onnect to 6b Picket top, page 56.

6a
Sunflowers and Crows
Picket (bottom)
Cut 1

7
Sunflowers and Crows
Picket
Cut 1

8
Sunflowers and Crows
Picket
Cut 1

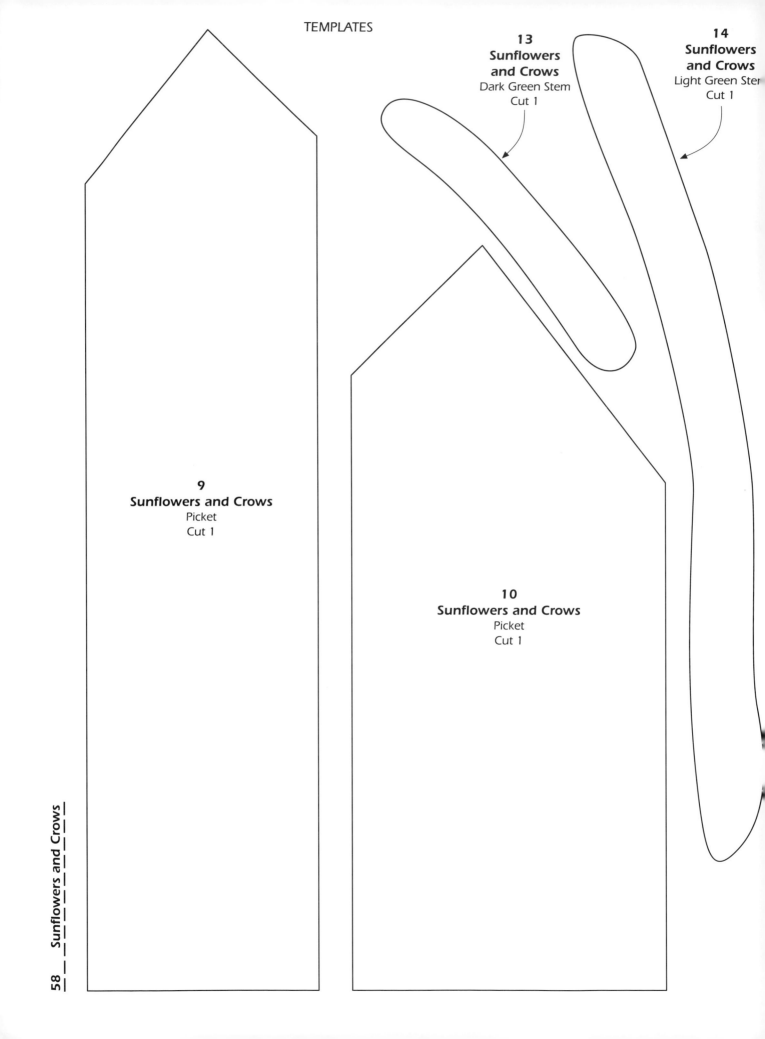

13
Sunflowers
and Crows
Dark Green Stem
Cut 1

14
Sunflowers
and Crows
Light Green Stem
Cut 1

9
Sunflowers and Crows
Picket
Cut 1

10
Sunflowers and Crows
Picket
Cut 1

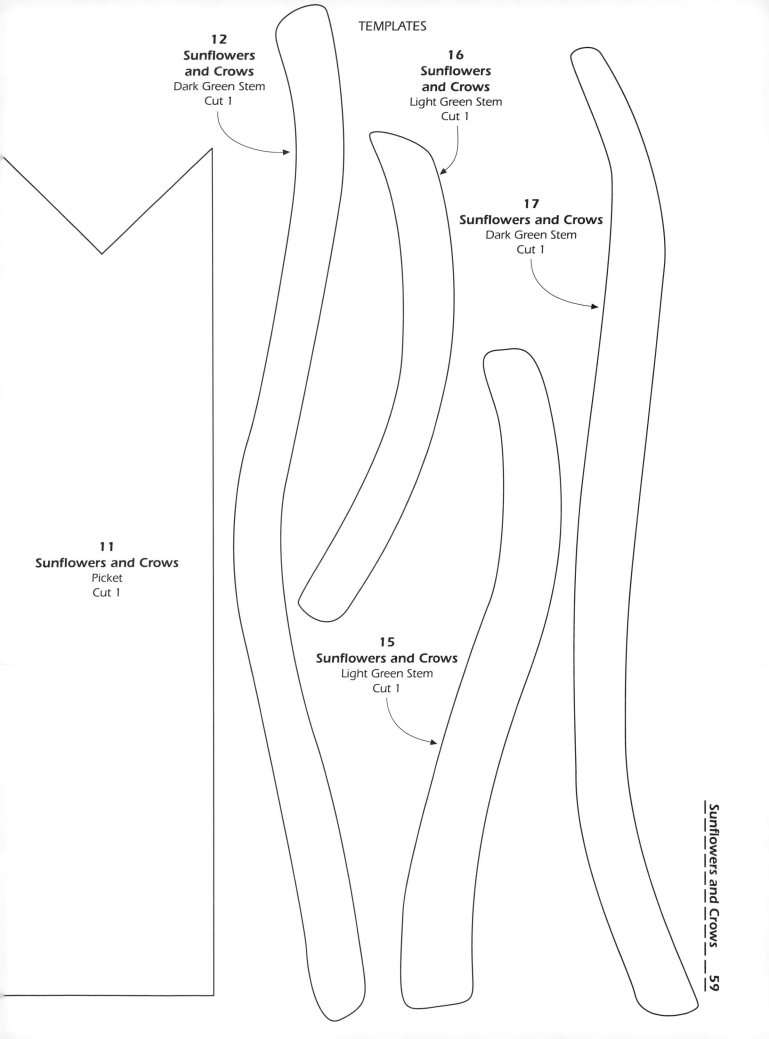

**12
Sunflowers
and Crows**
Dark Green Stem
Cut 1

**16
Sunflowers
and Crows**
Light Green Stem
Cut 1

**17
Sunflowers and Crows**
Dark Green Stem
Cut 1

**11
Sunflowers and Crows**
Picket
Cut 1

**15
Sunflowers and Crows**
Light Green Stem
Cut 1

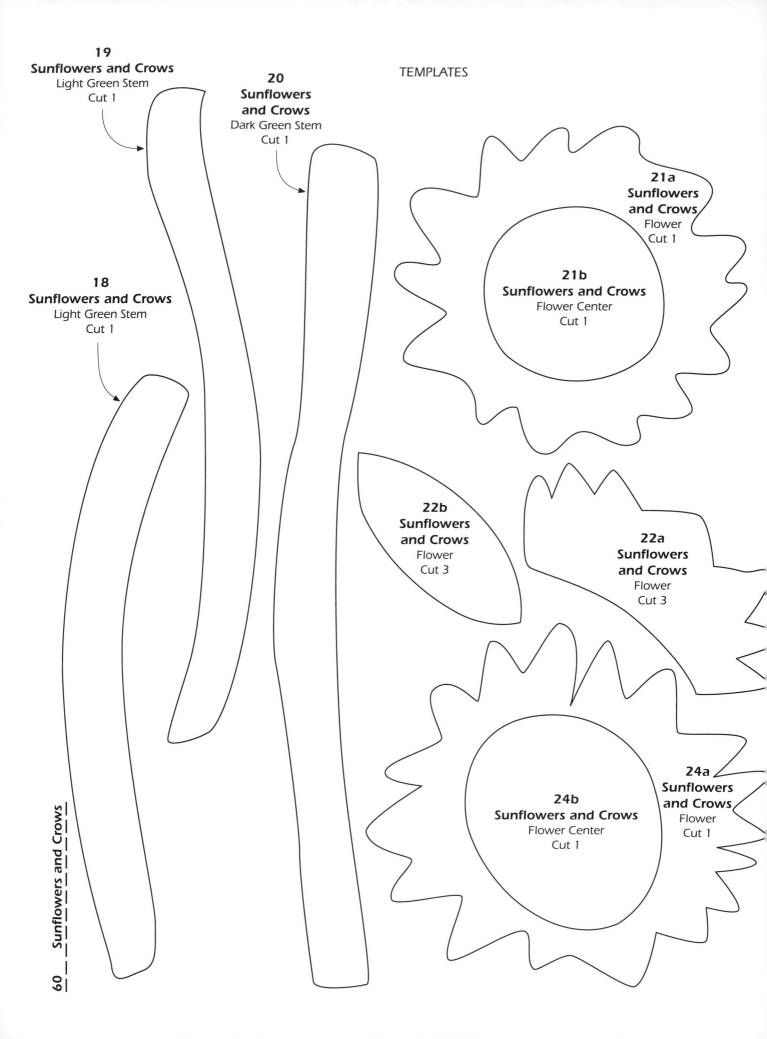

19
Sunflowers and Crows
Light Green Stem
Cut 1

20
Sunflowers and Crows
Dark Green Stem
Cut 1

18
Sunflowers and Crows
Light Green Stem
Cut 1

21a
Sunflowers and Crows
Flower
Cut 1

21b
Sunflowers and Crows
Flower Center
Cut 1

22b
Sunflowers and Crows
Flower
Cut 3

22a
Sunflowers and Crows
Flower
Cut 3

24b
Sunflowers and Crows
Flower Center
Cut 1

24a
Sunflowers and Crows
Flower
Cut 1

TEMPLATES

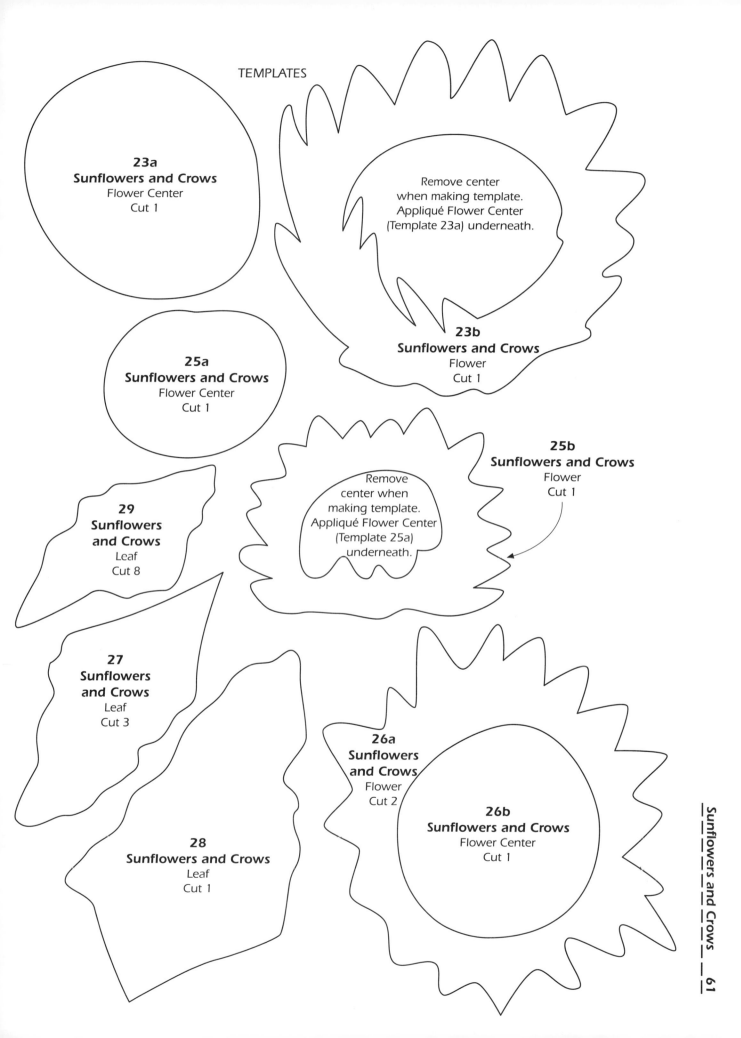

23a
Sunflowers and Crows
Flower Center
Cut 1

Remove center
when making template.
Appliqué Flower Center
(Template 23a) underneath.

23b
Sunflowers and Crows
Flower
Cut 1

25a
Sunflowers and Crows
Flower Center
Cut 1

25b
Sunflowers and Crows
Flower
Cut 1

Remove
center when
making template.
Appliqué Flower Center
(Template 25a)
underneath.

29
**Sunflowers
and Crows**
Leaf
Cut 8

27
**Sunflowers
and Crows**
Leaf
Cut 3

26a
**Sunflowers
and Crows**
Flower
Cut 2

26b
Sunflowers and Crows
Flower Center
Cut 1

28
Sunflowers and Crows
Leaf
Cut 1

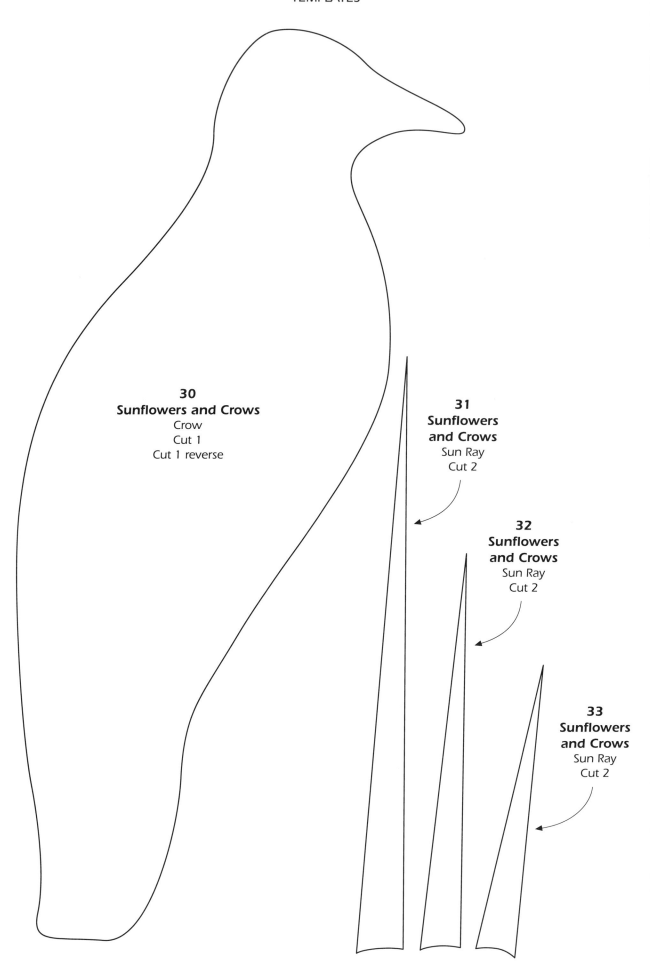

30
Sunflowers and Crows
Crow
Cut 1
Cut 1 reverse

31
Sunflowers
and Crows
Sun Ray
Cut 2

32
Sunflowers
and Crows
Sun Ray
Cut 2

33
Sunflowers
and Crows
Sun Ray
Cut 2

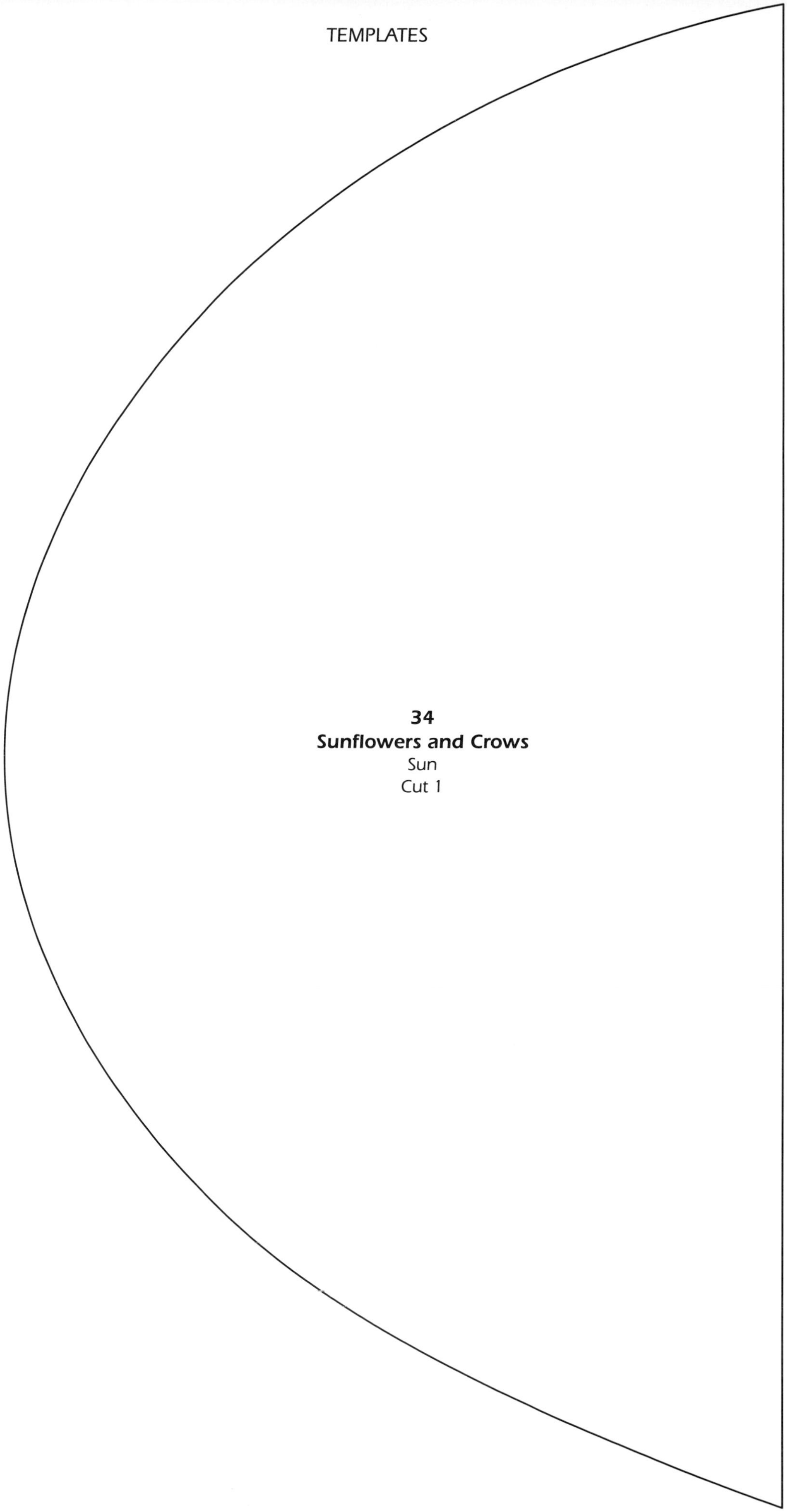

34
Sunflowers and Crows
Sun
Cut 1

Mittens and Snowmen

Snowmen are not just a symbol of Christmas—they can decorate your home all winter long.

Color Photo: page 22
Size: 28" x 36"
Materials: 44"-wide fabric

½ yd. muslin for Snowmen and Mitten blocks

⅜ yd. red checked (tiny checks) fabric for mittens and border

⅜ yd. red-white-and-blue plaid for mittens, Mitten blocks, hatband, moon, and border

⅜ yd. navy blue checked (tiny checks) fabric for mittens, Snowman block, small snowman's scarf, and border

⅜ yd. navy blue plaid for Snowman block, mittens, and border

⅛ yd. total of 2 red plaids or scraps of red fabric for mittens and small snowman's cap

¼ yd. navy blue solid for binding

32" x 40" piece of Pellon fleece or other thin batting

32" x 40" piece of fabric for backing

Black scrap for hat

#3 perle cotton in red or blue for pom-pom

#8 perle cotton in assorted colors, including black

1 yd. jute

1 white pom-pom

2 large red pom-poms

Chenille needle

2 ceramic star buttons for large Snowman block

2 ceramic snowman buttons for Mitten blocks

Assorted beads and buttons for snowmen's eyes and buttons

Carrot button for large snowman's nose

Small bells for hatband on large snowman

4 small wooden clothespins

Making the Foundation

Cutting

All seams are 1/4" wide.

From the muslin, cut:
- 1 rectangle, 8½" x 24½", for the Four-Mittens block
- 1 rectangle, 8½" x 16½", for the Double-Mitten block
- 1 square, 8½" x 8½", for a Single-Mitten block

From the red checked fabric, cut:
- 1 square, 8½" x 8½", for a Single-Mitten block
- 1 strip, 2½" x 36½", for right border

From the red-white-and-blue plaid, cut:
- 2 squares, each 8½" x 8½", for the Single-Mitten block
- 1 strip, 2½" x 26½", for top border

From the navy blue checked fabric, cut:
- 1 rectangle, 8½" x 16½", for the large Snowman block
- 1 strip, 2½" x 34½", for left border

From the navy blue plaid, cut:
- 1 square, 8½" x 8½", for the small Snowman block
- 1 strip, 2½" x 24½", for bottom border

Directions

1. Layer the batting on the backing. See "Making the Quilt Sandwich Foundation" on page 8.

2. Place the 8½" x 16½" navy blue checked rectangle lengthwise in the center of the batting. The shorter sides of the batting should be at the top and bottom. Set aside.

3. With right sides together, machine stitch the 8½" x 8½" red checked square to an 8½" x 8½" red-white-and-blue plaid square. Press. You now have a rectangle, 8½" x 16½".

4. Place the resulting unit along the left side of the navy blue checked rectangle on the batting with the red-white-and-blue square at the top. Next, place them right sides together, matching the left edges. Pin in place. Machine stitch through all the layers.

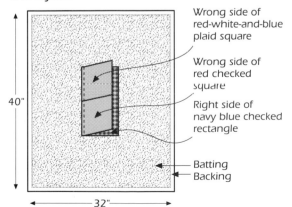

Wrong side of red-white-and-blue plaid square

Wrong side of red checked square

Right side of navy blue checked rectangle

Batting
Backing

40"

32"

5. Flip the squares/rectangle unit onto the batting. Press.

6. With right sides together, sew the 8½" x 8½" muslin square to the remaining 8½" x 8½" red-white-and-blue plaid square. Press.

7. Place the resulting unit along the right side of the navy blue checked rectangle. Next, place them right sides together, matching the right edges. Make sure that the red-white-and-blue square is toward the bottom of the quilt. Pin in place. Machine stitch through all the layers. Flip the squares/rectangle unit onto the batting. Press. Your quilt-top foundation should look like the illustration below.

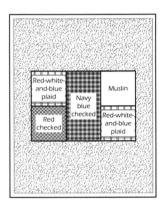

8. Pin the 8½" x 24½" muslin rectangle to the lower side of the units, right sides together. Stitch through all the layers. Flip the muslin rectangle onto the batting. Press.

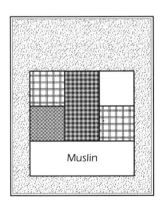

9. With right sides together, sew the 8½" x 8½" navy blue plaid square to the 8½" x 16½" muslin rectangle along one short side. Press the seam toward the darker fabric.

10. With right sides together, pin the unit made in step 9 to the upper edge of the units on the batting. Stitch through all the layers. Flip the unit onto the batting. Press.

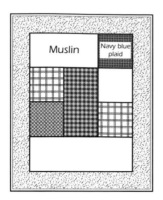

11. Add the borders, beginning with the bottom border. With right sides together, stitch the navy blue plaid border strip to the bottom edge. Flip the border onto the batting. Press.

12. Repeat the same procedure to add the navy blue checked border strip to the left side of the quilt. In a clockwise direction, add the top and then the right border. Be sure to press after adding each border.

13. Machine or hand quilt in-the-ditch along the seams where the border strips meet the inner blocks.

14. Bind the edges with 1½"-wide strips of solid navy blue fabric, following the directions on page 11.

Appliquilt

Use the templates on pages 67–69.

1. Make plastic templates for the large snowman, small snowman, hat, cap, scarf, large heart, small heart, large mitten, and small mitten. Directions for making templates are on page 9.

2. From the fabrics noted in the "Materials" list, cut:

   1 large snowman and 1 small snowman from muslin

   1 large mitten, 3 large hearts, and 1 small heart from the red checked fabric

   1 cap and a contrasting cap band, 1 hat and a contrasting hatband, 1 matching pair of large mittens, 1 large mitten, 1 small mitten, 2 large hearts, and 1 small heart from the red plaids

   1 small mitten, 1 small heart, and the moon from the red-white-and-blue plaid

   1 small heart and the small snowman's scarf from the navy blue checked fabric

   1 large heart from the navy blue plaid

3. Stitch the large snowman, then his hat, and then the hatband in place. Next, stitch the small snowman, his cap, then the cap band. Use contrasting colors of perle cotton. See Appliquilting directions on page 10.

4. Stitch the large and small mitten in place, referring to the quilt plan for placement. Then stitch large hearts to large mittens and small hearts to small mittens. Place contrasting fabric hearts on the mittens. For instance, if a mitten is primarily blue, stitch a red plaid heart to it.

5. Stitch the moon to the large Snowman block.

Embellishments

1. Attach the small snowman's scarf to his body with 2 rows of running stitches where his head meets his body, gathering it a bit as you go. Then "trail" it to the side, securing it in 3 spots with double knots.

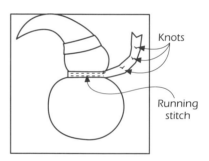

2. Stitch a small white pom-pom to the point of the small snowman's cap.

3. Attach 1 red pom-pom to a 32" length of #3 perle cotton (or yarn). Thread a chenille needle with the perle cotton. Beginning in one mitten, leave 3" of slack and insert the needle into the top of the mitten; make a double knot. Then sew along the top edge of the mitten with a running stitch. When you get to the end of the mitten top, bring the needle from the back side of the quilt to the front and make a double knot. Leave 6" of slack and then insert the needle into the top of the next mitten. Make a double knot, then sew across the top of that mitten using a running stitch. Bring the needle from the back side of the quilt to the front when you reach the edge of the mitten. Make a double knot. Leave 3" of slack, then sew another red pom-pom to that end of the perle cotton.

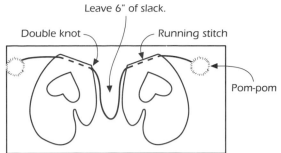

Double knot — Leave 6" of slack. — Running stitch

Pom-pom

4. Lay the jute along the top of the row of 4 mittens, leaving a tail at each end. With invisible nylon or matching thread, sew over the jute with a wide zigzag stitch to attach it to the quilt. You now have a clothesline! Use muslin-colored perle cotton thread to attach the clothespins just above each mitten.

5. Sew the star buttons onto the large Snowman block. Sew a snowman button to one large heart and to the block of another large mitten. Directions for sewing on buttons appear on page 12.

6. Finish embellishing the large snowman by attaching buttons for his "coat," beads for eyes, the carrot button for his nose, and bells on his hatband. Use a stem stitch and black perle cotton to add "branches" for his arms. Directions for embroidery stitches appear on page 12.

7. Embellish the small snowman with black beads for eyes and red beads for his "coat."

8. If you wish to embellish borders with triangles in a mock Flying Geese pattern, simply cut half-square triangles from 2" squares of scraps. Trim with pinking shears and stitch to borders as desired.

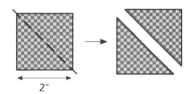

2"

Cut once diagonally.

Experiment and let your imagination go wild. Try different colors and placements of the pieces.

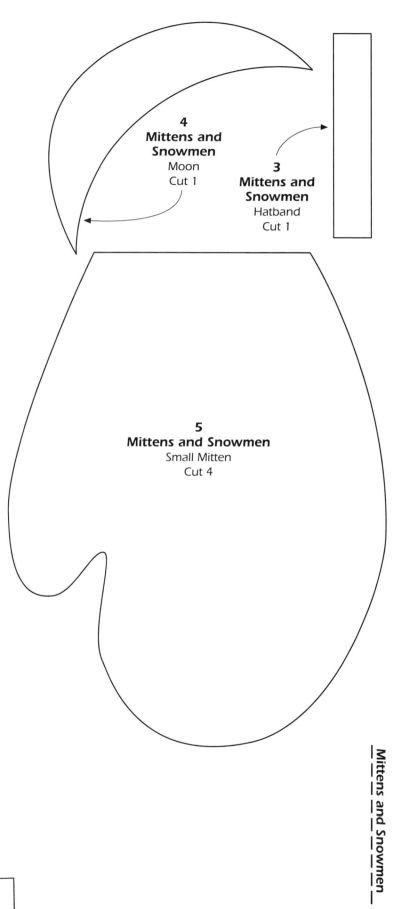

4
Mittens and Snowmen
Moon
Cut 1

3
Mittens and Snowmen
Hatband
Cut 1

5
Mittens and Snowmen
Small Mitten
Cut 4

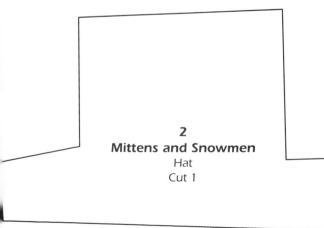

2
Mittens and Snowmen
Hat
Cut 1

6
Mittens and Snowmen
Small Heart
Cut 4

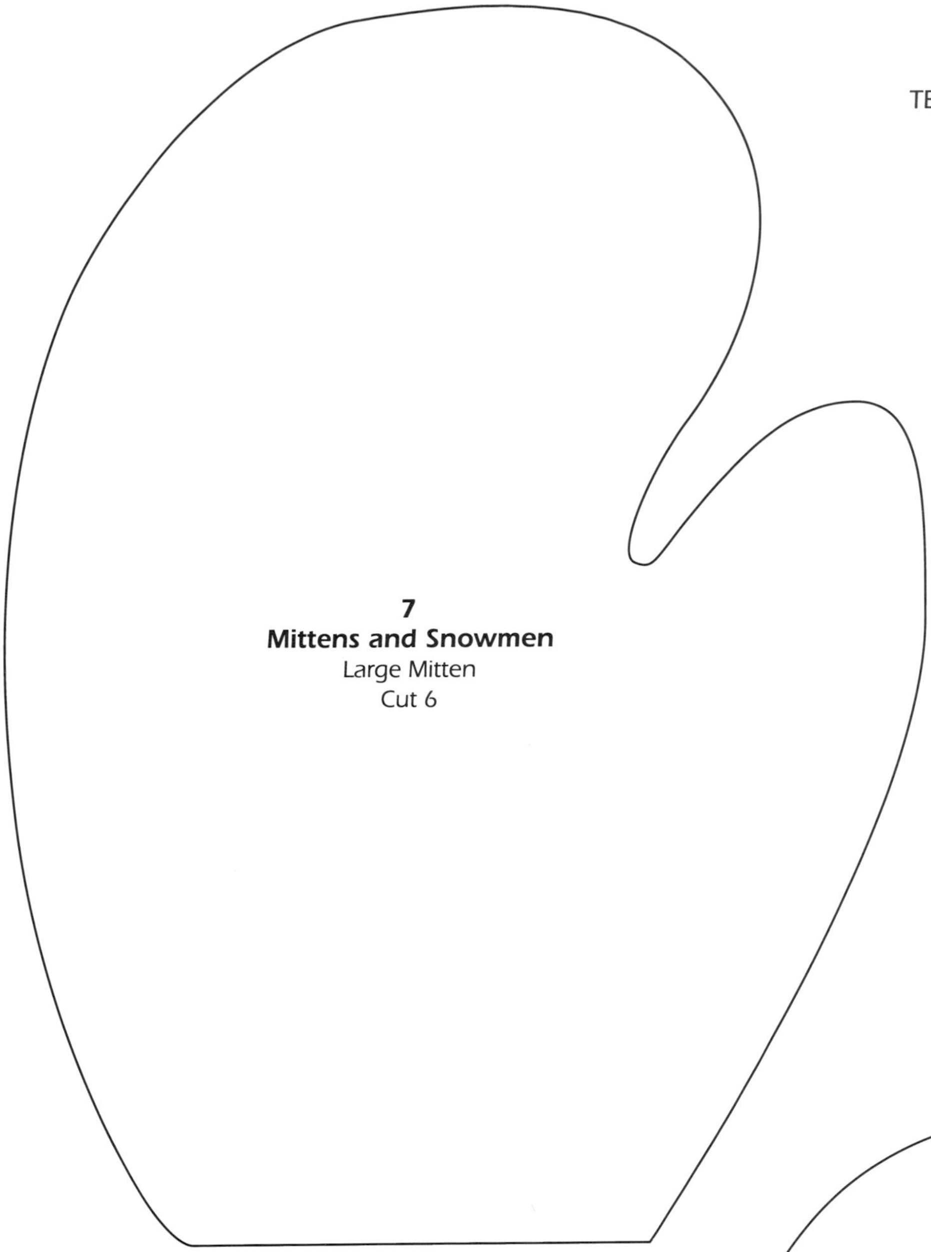

7
Mittens and Snowmen
Large Mitten
Cut 6

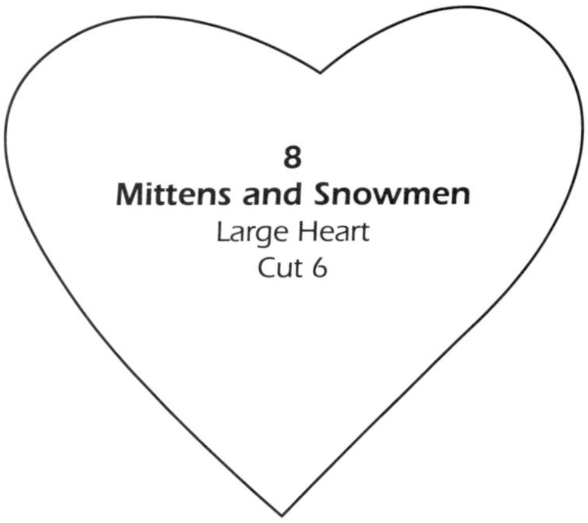

8
Mittens and Snowmen
Large Heart
Cut 6

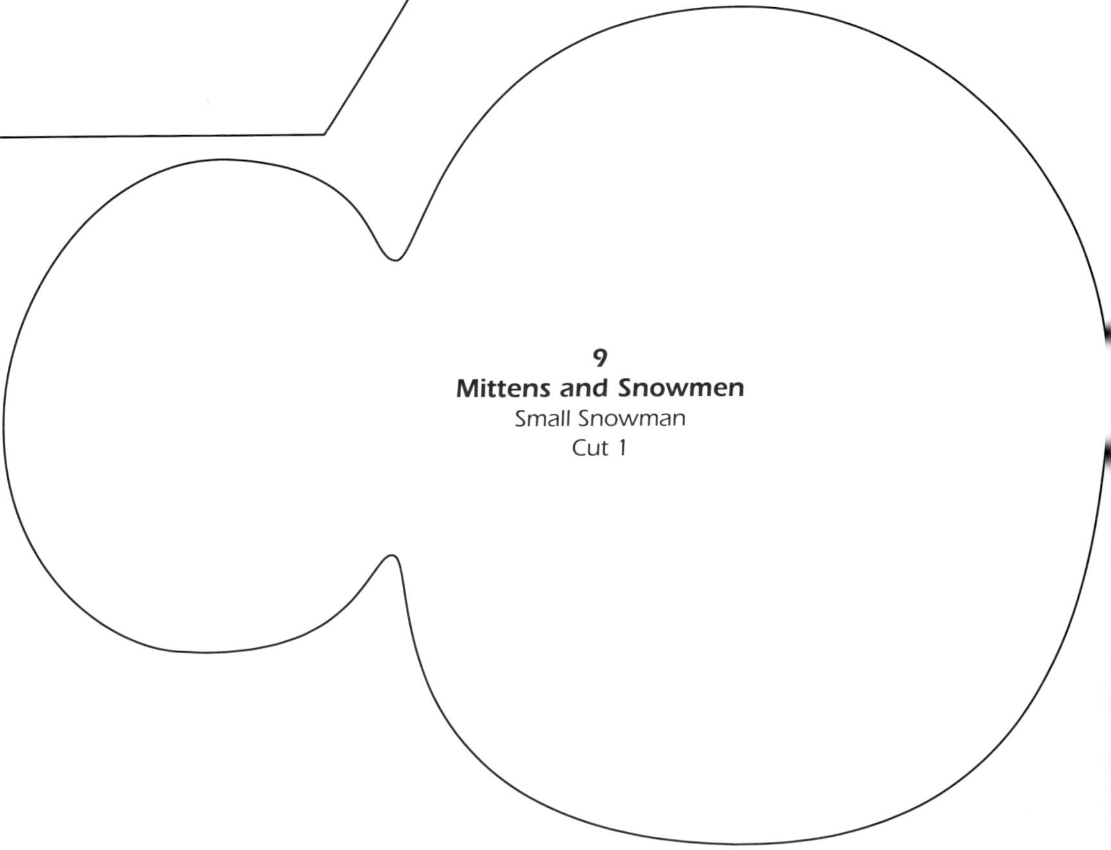

9
Mittens and Snowmen
Small Snowman
Cut 1

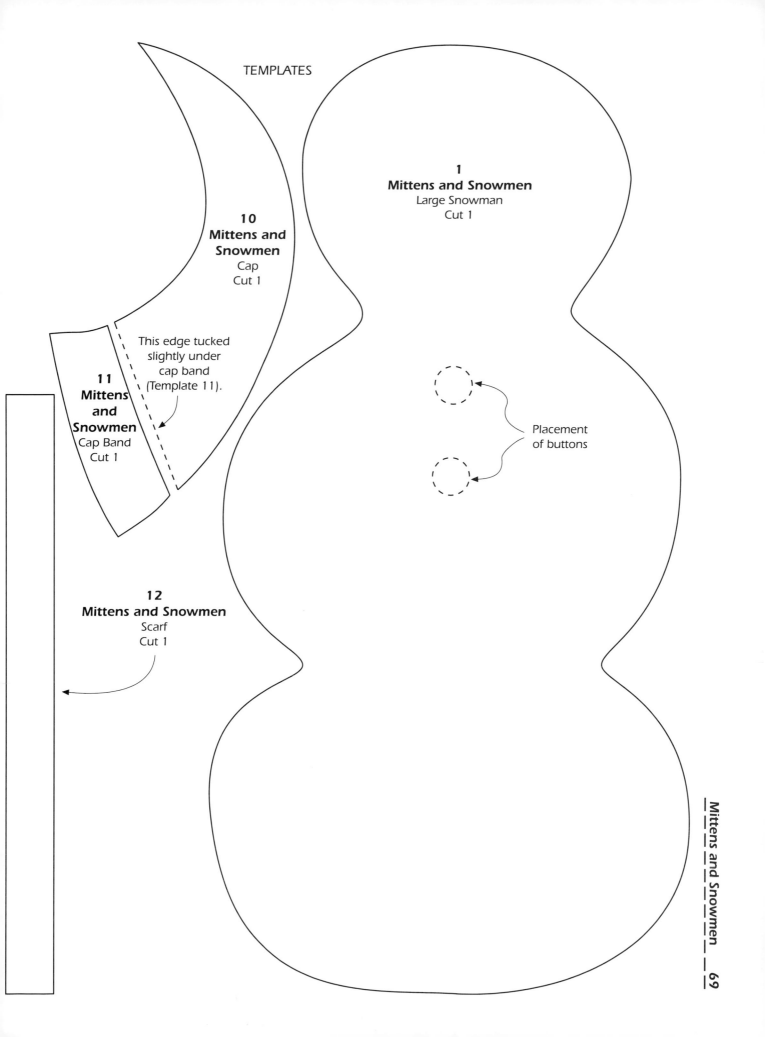

TEMPLATES

10
Mittens and Snowmen
Cap
Cut 1

1
Mittens and Snowmen
Large Snowman
Cut 1

This edge tucked slightly under cap band (Template 11).

11
Mittens and Snowmen
Cap Band
Cut 1

Placement of buttons

12
Mittens and Snowmen
Scarf
Cut 1

How Does Your Garden Grow?

Bring out your scrap basket, as this quilt is a great way to use some of your leftover pieces. Anything goes—solid-colored fabrics, small prints, plaids, and large prints. Make your own favorite vegetables and "plant" them in your garden.

Color Photo: page 17
Size: 44" x 41"
Materials: 44"-wide fabric

1¼ yds. dark fabric (brown or black) for background "patches" in the garden

1⅛ yds. striped fabric for lattice (sashing between and around the garden patches)

½ yd. brown-and-black print for border

⅜ yd. dark brown-and-black striped fabric for binding or same striped fabric as used for lattice

⅛–¼ yd. each or scraps of the following:
    Yellow for corn and squash
    Light green for squash
    3 different greens for stems and leaves
    3 different beiges or browns for mushrooms
    Green for asparagus
    2 different greens for peas
    2 different purples for eggplants
    2 different reds for pepper
    Green for pepper
    Green for carrot tops
    Orange for carrots
    2 different greens for watermelon
    Pink for watermelon
    Assorted reds for tomatoes
    Orange for pumpkin
    Blue for bird
    2 different greens for cabbage
    Brown wood-grain print fabric for sign placards and posts
    Muslin for signs

#8 perle cotton in assorted colors, including yellow

8"-long piece of green jute for pea vine

13 green buttons for peas

Embellishments of your choice, such as ladybug buttons, corn buttons, seed-packet buttons, a miniature birdhouse, and miniature garden tools

Making the Foundation
Cutting

Refer to the Garden Patch Cutting Plan at right for the measurements of each "patch" in the garden. Each patch is labeled with the name of the vegetable that is growing in it. The measurements shown are the cut size and include the 1/4"-wide seam allowances all around.

1. From the dark fabric and following the Garden Patch Cutting Plan, cut the backgrounds for each patch.
2. From the lattice fabric, cut:
   2 strips, crosswise, each 2½" x 38½", for lattice strips
   4 strips, lengthwise, each 2½" x 31½", for lattice strips

You will cut additional 2½"-wide lattice strips into the required lengths as you join garden patches during the foundation construction.

3. From the dark brown, cut:
   2 strips, each 3½" x 35½", for the side borders
   2 strips, each 3½" x 44½", for the top and bottom borders

Directions

All seams are 1/4" wide.
Refer to the Garden Patch Construction Plan at right.

1. With right sides together, sew the corn, mushroom, and asparagus patches together with 2½" x 5½" lattice strips between them, as shown in the Garden Patch Construction Plan for Unit 1. Press. This unit should measure 5½" x 31½".
2. With right sides together, sew the pea, eggplant, and pepper patches together with 2½" x 8½" lattice strips between them, as shown in the construction plan for Unit 2. Press. This unit should measure 8½" x 31½".
3. With right sides together, sew the bottom edge of the carrot patch to a 2½" x 17½" lattice strip for Unit 3 as shown in the construction plan. Press. This unit should now measure 8½" x 17½".
4. With right sides together, sew the watermelon and pumpkin patches together with a 2½" x 10½" lattice strip between them. Press. The result should measure 10½" x 16½". Next, add a 2½" x 16½" lattice strip and the tomato patch to create Unit 4. This unit should measure 17½" x 16½".
5. With right sides together, sew the squash and cabbage patches together, with a 2½" x 5½" lattice strip between them. Press. The result should measure 5½" x 17½". Next, add a 2½" x 17½" lattice strip to the top edge for Unit 5. This unit should now measure 7½" x 17½".

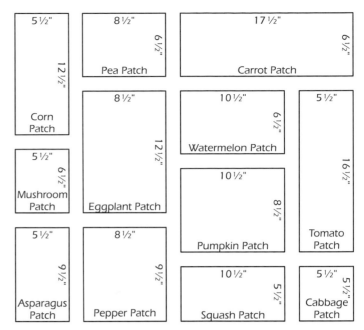

The measurements shown include 1/4"-wide seam allowances.

Garden Patch Cutting Plan

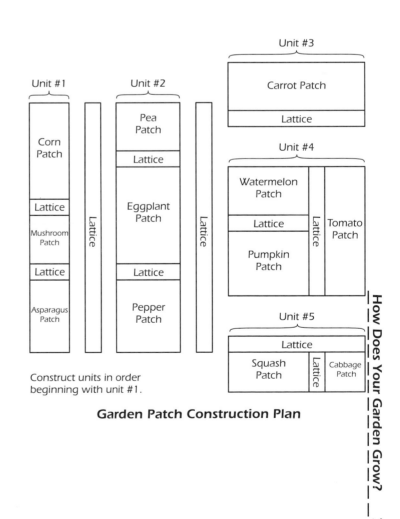

Construct units in order beginning with unit #1.

Garden Patch Construction Plan

6. Sew the bottom edge of Unit 3 to the top edge of Unit 4 . Then sew the top edge of Unit 5 to the bottom edge of Unit 4. Press the seams. This should now measure 17½" x 31½".

7. Join the completed units with 2½" x 31½" lattice strips between them as shown. Add the remaining 2½" x 31½" lattice strips to the sides of the quilt top. Press. Sew 2½" x 38½" lattice strips to the top and bottom edges. Press.

8. Sew the 3½" x 35½" border strips to the sides of the quilt top. Press.

9. Sew the 3½" x 44½" border strips to the top and bottom edge of the quilt. Press.

10. Now that the quilt top background is completed, layer it with the batting and backing. Baste the layers together. See "Making the Quilt Sandwich Foundation" on page 8.

11. Machine quilt in-the-ditch along the seam lines around all of the garden patches.

12. Bind the edges with 1½"-wide strips of striped fabric, following the directions on page 11.

Appliquilt

Use templates on pages 73–80.

1. Make plastic templates for the vegetables, following the directions on page 9.

2. Cut the vegetables from the scraps of fabrics as noted in the "Materials" list.

3. Stitch the vegetables to their appropriate patches in the order indicated by the numbered templates. Embellishments that add interest to the garden patches are noted below. Read through them before beginning to stitch. Refer to the quilt plan on page 70 for placement of the vegetables in their patches. See Appliquilting directions on page 10.

Embellishments

1. **Asparagus:** Following the lines that are drawn on the asparagus template, use straight stitches or crow footing and a contrasting perle cotton or floss to add texture to the asparagus tops.

2. **Peas:** Sew buttons in contrasting shades of green to the pea pods. Lay the vine of green jute along the tops of the pea pods, as shown in the quilt plan. Tack down the jute using the couching method (page 51), or use a machine zigzag stitch and invisible thread.

3. **Carrots:** Make carrot tops from green fabrics, following the directions on page 35. Stitch them to the quilt along the bottom strip edges with a short row of stitches before sewing the carrots in place. Secure the strips to the quilt by making a single stitch at the top and in the middle of each strip. Tie each stitch with a double knot.

4. **Pumpkins:** Stitch, following the lines that are drawn on the pumpkin template. This adds the creases to the pumpkin.

5. **Squash:** Cut the squash stems separately in a darker color (brown or green). Refer to the squash template for placement of the stems.

6. **Cabbage:** Stitch the cabbage leaves to the quilt, following the lines on the cabbage template. Draw your own lines or follow the transfer method outlined for the God Bless America quilt on page 50.

7. **Bird:** With yellow perle cotton, use a stem stitch (page 12) to make the bird's legs. Draw your own lines or follow the transfer method on page 50. Make a French knot (page 12) or attach a bead for the bird's eye.

8. **Earthworms:** From green fabric, cut earthworms and stitch them to the quilt. I stitched one to the bird's mouth and one to the lattice next to the tomato patch. Add French knots for eyes or use a marker to draw them.

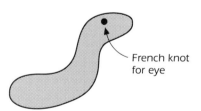

French knot for eye

9. **Signs, signposts, and placards:** From the brown wood-grain fabric, cut the signposts and placards. Cut the signs from muslin. Use a permanent marker to print "HOW DOES YOUR GARDEN GROW," writing one word on each muslin sign board as shown on the templates. Center each of the signs on top of the sign placards. Stitch them to the quilt after stitching the posts.

10. Add other embellishments, such as small wooden vegetables tied with jute or raffia, tiny garden tools, and buttons.

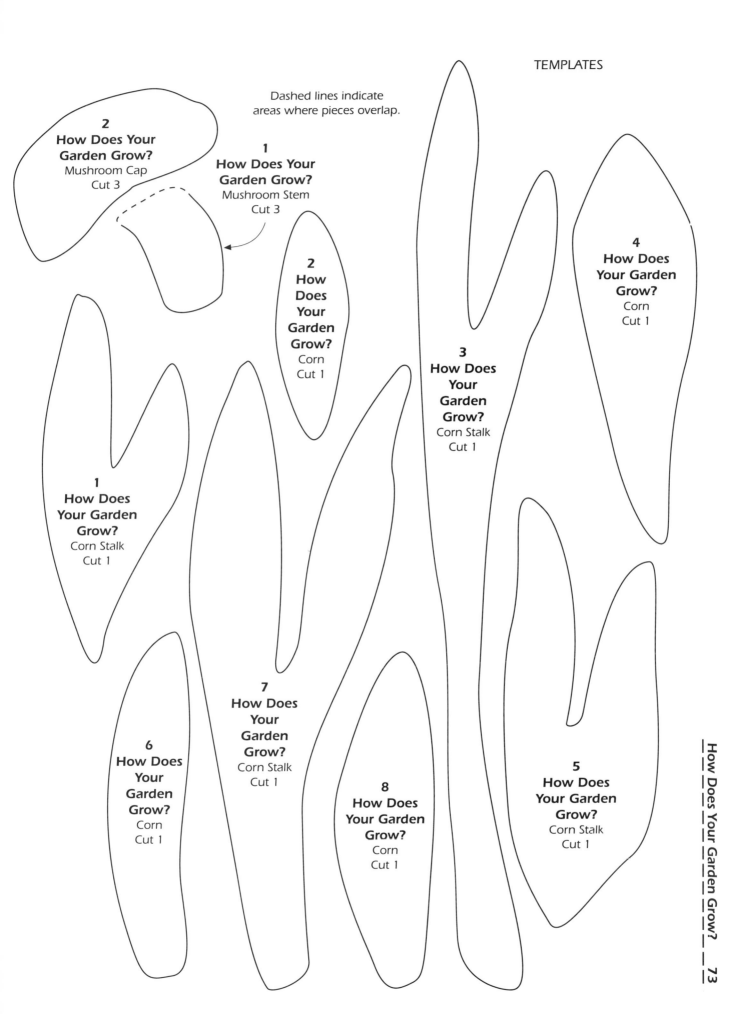

TEMPLATES

Dashed lines indicate
areas where pieces overlap.

2
**How Does Your
Garden Grow?**
Mushroom Cap
Cut 3

1
**How Does Your
Garden Grow?**
Mushroom Stem
Cut 3

2
**How
Does
Your
Garden
Grow?**
Corn
Cut 1

4
**How Does
Your Garden
Grow?**
Corn
Cut 1

3
**How Does
Your
Garden
Grow?**
Corn Stalk
Cut 1

1
**How Does
Your Garden
Grow?**
Corn Stalk
Cut 1

7
**How Does
Your
Garden
Grow?**
Corn Stalk
Cut 1

6
**How Does
Your
Garden
Grow?**
Corn
Cut 1

8
**How Does
Your Garden
Grow?**
Corn
Cut 1

5
**How Does
Your Garden
Grow?**
Corn Stalk
Cut 1

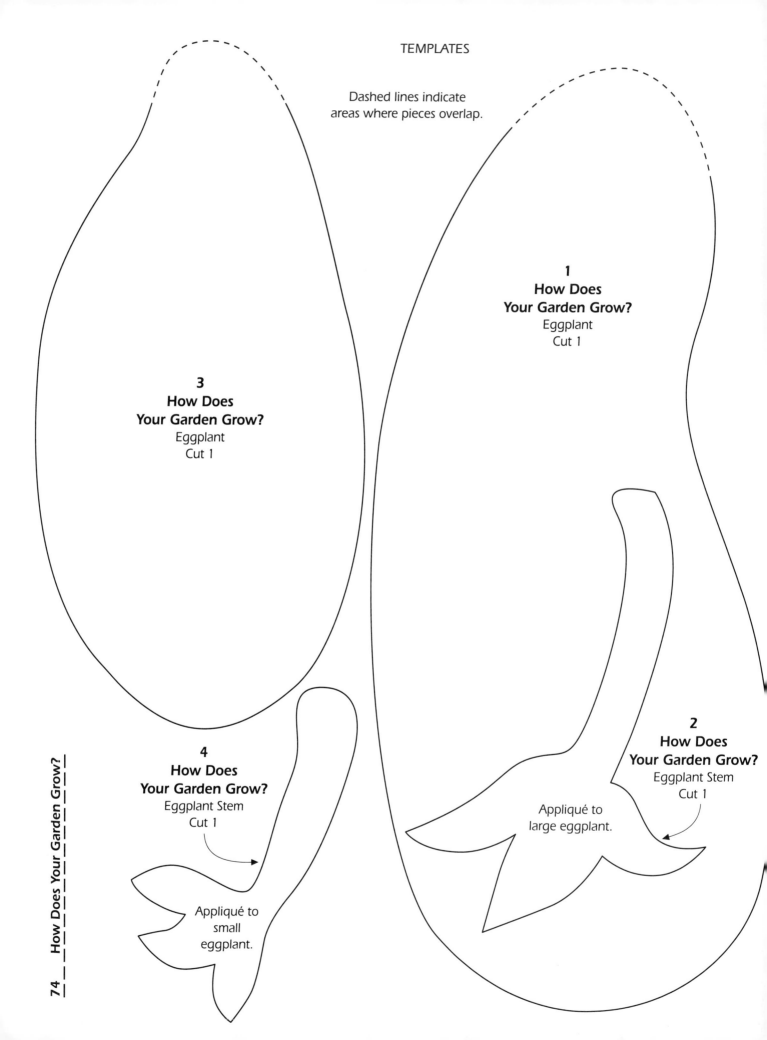

TEMPLATES

Dashed lines indicate
areas where pieces overlap.

1
**How Does
Your Garden Grow?**
Eggplant
Cut 1

3
**How Does
Your Garden Grow?**
Eggplant
Cut 1

2
**How Does
Your Garden Grow?**
Eggplant Stem
Cut 1

Appliqué to
large eggplant.

4
**How Does
Your Garden Grow?**
Eggplant Stem
Cut 1

Appliqué to
small
eggplant.

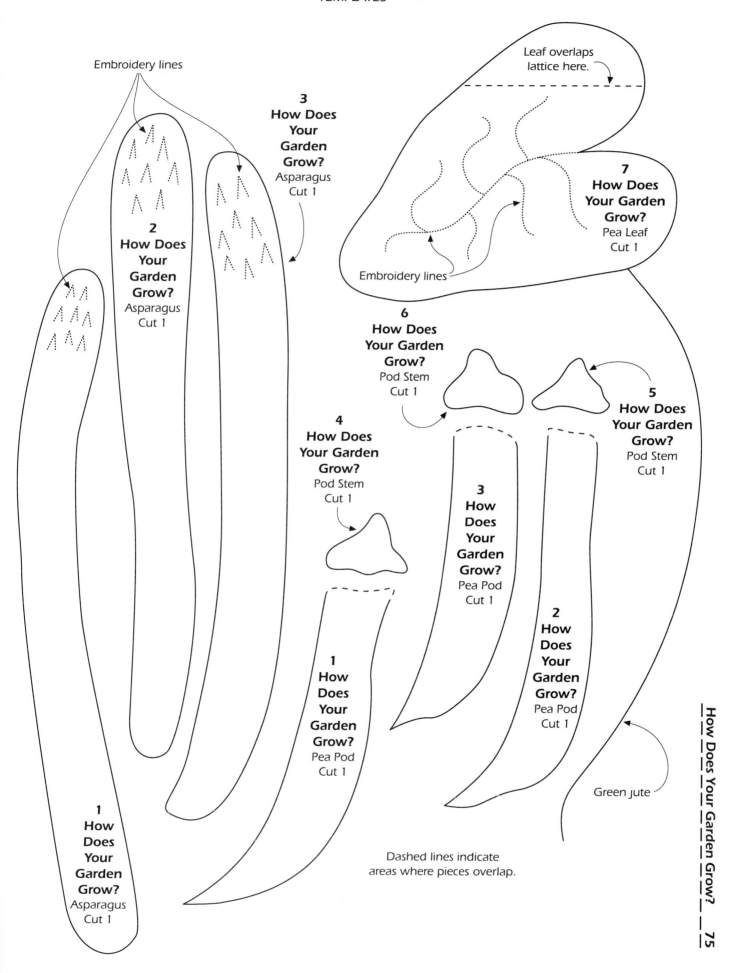

Embroidery lines

Leaf overlaps
lattice here.

3
How Does
Your
Garden
Grow?
Asparagus
Cut 1

7
How Does
Your Garden
Grow?
Pea Leaf
Cut 1

2
How Does
Your
Garden
Grow?
Asparagus
Cut 1

Embroidery lines

6
How Does
Your Garden
Grow?
Pod Stem
Cut 1

5
How Does
Your Garden
Grow?
Pod Stem
Cut 1

4
How Does
Your Garden
Grow?
Pod Stem
Cut 1

3
How
Does
Your
Garden
Grow?
Pea Pod
Cut 1

2
How
Does
Your
Garden
Grow?
Pea Pod
Cut 1

1
How
Does
Your
Garden
Grow?
Pea Pod
Cut 1

1
How
Does
Your
Garden
Grow?
Asparagus
Cut 1

Dashed lines indicate
areas where pieces overlap.

Green jute

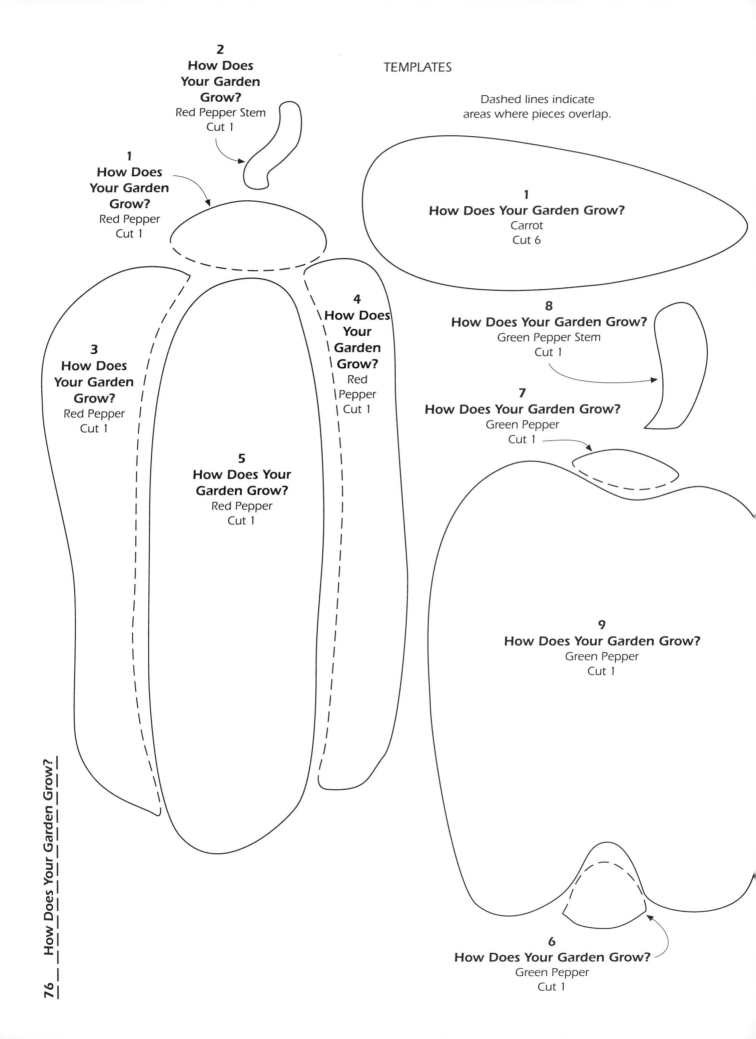

2
How Does Your Garden Grow?
Red Pepper Stem
Cut 1

TEMPLATES

Dashed lines indicate areas where pieces overlap.

1
How Does Your Garden Grow?
Red Pepper
Cut 1

1
How Does Your Garden Grow?
Carrot
Cut 6

4
How Does Your Garden Grow?
Red Pepper
Cut 1

3
How Does Your Garden Grow?
Red Pepper
Cut 1

8
How Does Your Garden Grow?
Green Pepper Stem
Cut 1

7
How Does Your Garden Grow?
Green Pepper
Cut 1

5
How Does Your Garden Grow?
Red Pepper
Cut 1

9
How Does Your Garden Grow?
Green Pepper
Cut 1

6
How Does Your Garden Grow?
Green Pepper
Cut 1

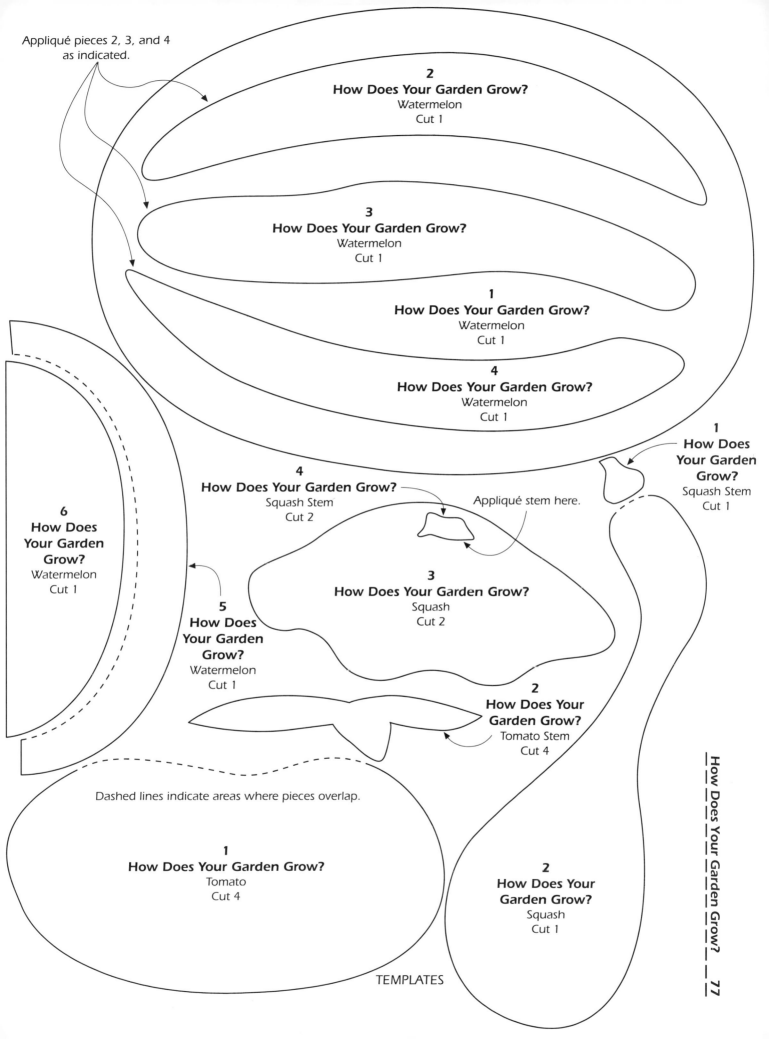

Appliqué pieces 2, 3, and 4 as indicated.

2
How Does Your Garden Grow?
Watermelon
Cut 1

3
How Does Your Garden Grow?
Watermelon
Cut 1

1
How Does Your Garden Grow?
Watermelon
Cut 1

4
How Does Your Garden Grow?
Watermelon
Cut 1

1
How Does Your Garden Grow?
Squash Stem
Cut 1

4
How Does Your Garden Grow?
Squash Stem
Cut 2

Appliqué stem here.

6
How Does Your Garden Grow?
Watermelon
Cut 1

3
How Does Your Garden Grow?
Squash
Cut 2

5
How Does Your Garden Grow?
Watermelon
Cut 1

2
How Does Your Garden Grow?
Tomato Stem
Cut 4

Dashed lines indicate areas where pieces overlap.

1
How Does Your Garden Grow?
Tomato
Cut 4

2
How Does Your Garden Grow?
Squash
Cut 1

TEMPLATES

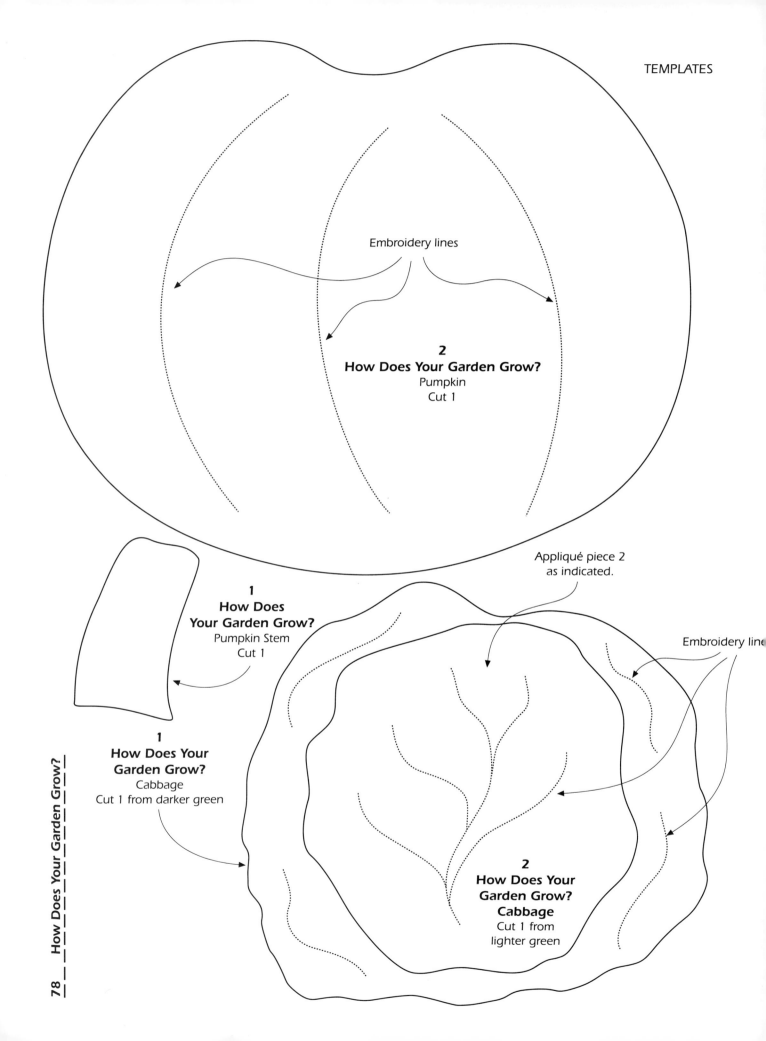

Embroidery lines

2
How Does Your Garden Grow?
Pumpkin
Cut 1

Appliqué piece 2
as indicated.

Embroidery line

1
**How Does
Your Garden Grow?**
Pumpkin Stem
Cut 1

1
**How Does Your
Garden Grow?**
Cabbage
Cut 1 from darker green

2
**How Does Your
Garden Grow?**
Cabbage
Cut 1 from
lighter green

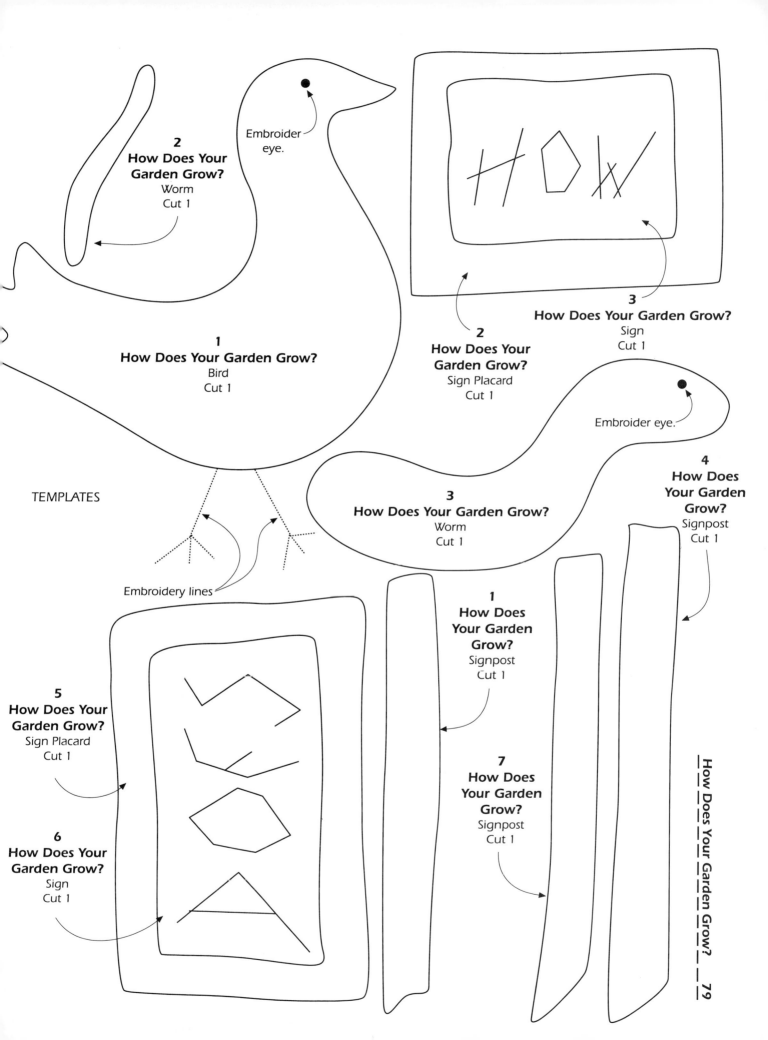

TEMPLATES

2
How Does Your Garden Grow?
Worm
Cut 1

Embroider eye.

1
How Does Your Garden Grow?
Bird
Cut 1

Embroidery lines

2
How Does Your Garden Grow?
Sign Placard
Cut 1

3
How Does Your Garden Grow?
Sign
Cut 1

Embroider eye.

3
How Does Your Garden Grow?
Worm
Cut 1

4
How Does Your Garden Grow?
Signpost
Cut 1

1
How Does Your Garden Grow?
Signpost
Cut 1

5
How Does Your Garden Grow?
Sign Placard
Cut 1

6
How Does Your Garden Grow?
Sign
Cut 1

7
How Does Your Garden Grow?
Signpost
Cut 1

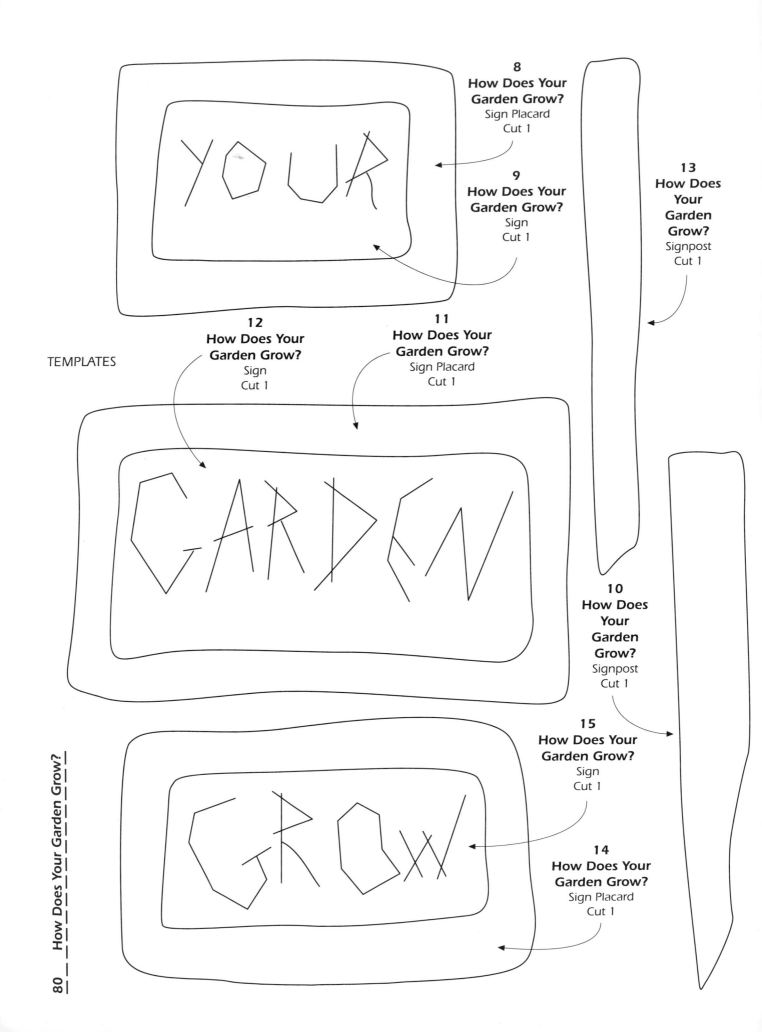

8
How Does Your Garden Grow?
Sign Placard
Cut 1

9
How Does Your Garden Grow?
Sign
Cut 1

13
How Does Your Garden Grow?
Signpost
Cut 1

12
How Does Your Garden Grow?
Sign
Cut 1

11
How Does Your Garden Grow?
Sign Placard
Cut 1

10
How Does Your Garden Grow?
Signpost
Cut 1

15
How Does Your Garden Grow?
Sign
Cut 1

14
How Does Your Garden Grow?
Sign Placard
Cut 1